# Twin Flame Union

## The Ascension of
## St. Germain and Portia

**Claire Heartsong and Catherine Ann Clemett**

**LightRiver Media**

**Las Vegas, Nevada**

Cover Design: Magdalene Graphics, Sydney, Australia
Cover Image: Iscatel/Shuttershock

ISBN # 978-0-9847209-2-7

Library of Congress Control Number: 2014903116


LightRiver Media
889 S Rainbow Blvd. #598
Las Vegas, NV 89145

www.lightrivermedia.com
www.catherineannclemett.com

# Table of Contents

# Introduction

Thank you for joining us on the journey into greater understanding of Twin Souls and Twin Flames. Our journey's destination is Twin Flame Union - simple enough words, but the actual experience is beyond mental concepts. Our hope is that you will receive this book as an invitation and a catalyst from the Ascended Masters to consciously join with them in the realization of Twin Flame Union.

In this presentation two of these extraordinary beings are known as St Germain and Portia. There are other Masters who have attained Union on many inter-penetrating levels, as well. They all invite us into a process that heals separation consciousness/ perception, and the suffering that accompanies it, completely and absolutely. They reassure us that we are already realized Twin Flame Union consciousness; but our awareness of that truth is obscured by conditioned patterns of dualistic perception. Our journey involves skillfully and compassionately removing these obscurations. The destination is knowing and being the Oneness. Ultimately the goal and the path are inseparable.

Within these chapters you will be introduced to Claire Heartsong's and Catherine Ann Clemett's understanding of Twin Souls, Twin Flames and Twin Flame Union. We are aware that even though we are fully committed to this journey and its destination, what you will read can only reflect our limited experiences, fleeting glimpses and limited view. We humbly offer our understandings and thankfully, the more expanded consciousness of Anna, St Germain and Portia as it expressed through our human filters. Our aspiration is that these words, which only point to the destination, will awaken and support our collectively shared journey into Twin Flame realization. Any errors are ours and we pray that you will, without hindrance, gain direct access to the truth that will light your way, give your steps confidence and your heart constant comfort.

This book is a compilation of selected teachings that touch on the subject of Twin Souls, Twin Flames and Twin Flame Union. Much of the material is excerpted from the books *St. Germain: Twin-Souls & Soulmates* by Azena Ramanda and Claire Heartsong; *Anna, Grandmother of Jesus,* by Claire Heartsong; its sequel, *Anna, the Voice of the Magdalenes* by Claire Heartsong and Catherine Ann Clemett; *Soulweaving: Return to the Heart of the Mother* by Catherine Ann Clemett; and *BECOMING: 2011, Awakening the Great Human Potential* which is Anna material copyright by Claire Heartsong, translated and published in French by Ariane Editions, Inc., Montreal, Canada. The balance of the material is taken from transcriptions of public Anna presentations channeled by Claire Heartsong and often includes dialogue between Anna and participants. Claire and Catherine Ann have each written certain chapters.

# *Note of Clarification*

To clarify who has written what chapters, we have included symbols attached to each paragraph heading designating who wrote that chapter. Claire's symbol is ♥ and Catherine Ann's symbol is ♣ Footnotes for the excerpted material appear towards the end of the book so the reader will not be distracted. As a way of making the flow of the material more readable, we have also included our own personal writings which reflect our contemplations on this most wondrous subject so near and dear to our hearts.

May you receive the blessings and authentic empowerments that will result in your ascension into Twin Flame Union for the sake of all beings!

Namaste,

Claire Heartsong & Catherine Ann Clemett

# Part 1

## CHAPTER 1

## *St. Germain, the Catalyst*

### ♥ Claire's Meeting With St. Germain

In the fall of 1987, near a waterfall in the Grand Tetons, I experienced a completely life-transforming physical encounter with the ascended master St. Germain (previously Joseph, the father of Jesus, or Yeshua, as was his Aramaic name). Shortly thereafter, I was informed that I had a close connection with Yeshua's grandmother, the mother of Mary, also known as Anna of Mount Carmel.

Almost a year later while in deep meditation Anna appeared to me on the inner planes and said she desired to share her story with me. So it was then I began to experience Anna telepathically telling me about her life. I was also taken holographically into her experiences, which I then sporadically recorded over the next ten years. These preliminary experiences and writings laid the foundation for the book, *"Anna, Grandmother of Jesus."* After much purification on all levels, I began a disciplined course of writing in 1998 until

1

the book was published in 2002. While receiving transmissions from Anna during this time, it became clear that there was to be a sequel. Work on the sequel, *"Anna, the Voice of the Magdalenes"* began in 2006 and it was published in 2010. In 1990 Yeshua Sananda (the ascended Jesus) and St. Germain invited Allisone Heartsong, my then spiritual partner, and me to enter into a year of seclusion in which we experienced a profound and supremely intense "Twin-Flame" initiatory process. The experiences we shared during this time "apart from the world" still continue to open my spiritual View. I was deeply touched by the Divine Mother's Presence and by glimpses of St. Germain's and Portia's Twin Flame Union while in the "alchemical chrysalis," I shall forever be grateful to these beloved Masters for blessing me with their continuing guidance and holding me with their constant, caring compassion and love throughout this life and throughout all time.

## ♣ Catherine Ann's Meeting With St. Germain

I also had a physical encounter with St. Germain who appeared to me and a few friends as a bum in the Boston Common in 1982. I could have easily, at the time, passed off this extraordinary and life-changing encounter as an exchange with a crazy homeless person. However, many things said during the exchange, which made no sense to me at the time, continued to haunt and puzzle me. Over the next twenty-five year period of my life the significance of all of those seemingly crazy things which were said to me became clear bit-by-bit. The understanding unfolded like pieces to a puzzle.

Now I rarely talk to bums but there was something very magnetic about this bum. The first thing he said to me was, "Wouldn't it be nice to hang upside down and swing like a bat." I was thinking, yeah sure, whatever - I'm definitely think you're crazy. As the encounter with the bum proceeded, I kept having intense bodily sensations and reactions which were very puzzling to me. His conversation was intriguing, sometimes profoundly knowledgeable, other times astute and intuitive, but oftentimes it just didn't seem to make any sense. I began to suspect this "bum" might be an "ascended being". I had no idea, however, who he was or if, indeed, that was true.

A couple of years later the first puzzle piece became clear. In 1984, an acquaintance invited me to stop by and visit him if I were ever traveling up the Oregon Coast. One day I finally took him up on his offer and stopped to visit. He had an apartment up on a hill with a panoramic view of the ocean and Depoe Bay. He had recently purchased some gravity boots and was excited for me to try them. They were sort of like fiberglass ski boots with a big hook attached to the back. After pulling out the dresser drawers, so I could use them like steps to hoist my lower body up high enough to be able to hook the boots onto the bar in the doorway, I finally succeeded in getting them hooked to the bar. When I let go, I was hanging upside down. My friend gave me a push.

I found myself facing into his bedroom where, on the opposite wall, was a large four or five foot poster of some Master. I asked who it was. My friend said, "Oh that is St. Germain". Now I had never heard of him before. A short while later when I was trying to find out more about who St. Germain was, it suddenly dawned on me, the very first time I ever heard his name (in this life), I was "hanging upside down and swinging like a bat". This was the very first thing the bum in the Boston Common had said to me which seemed crazy at the time. I now had no doubt the "bum" I encountered two years earlier in Boston, was indeed, the Master St. Germain. For anyone interested in learning more about my experience with St. Germain, I share the full story of this encounter in my book *Soulweaving, Return to the Heart of the Mother.*

## ♣ The Master Plan Begins to Reveal Itself

I first read Claire's book, *Anna, Grandmother of Jesus*, 22 years after my encounter with St. Germain as the "bum". It was in the last chapter of *Anna, Grandmother of Jesus* titled, "A letter from Claire", that I first learned of Claire's life-changing experience with St. Germain similar to my own. This became the point of connection. I gathered up the courage to email Claire to see if she was willing to share more details about her encounter with St. Germain. This was the first time I had ever come across someone else who had also had an encounter with St. Germain in a physical body, rather than just experiencing him in a meditative state or in a channeling session.

When Claire and I finally shared the details of our encounters with St. Germain with one another, it became clear we both had made ourselves available for whatever was being asked of us. It also became clear that Anna, St. Germain and the Councils of Light had been busy, all along, guiding a much larger plan to unfold. St. Germain was the instigator for both of us.

The interaction between Claire and myself did not happen right away with that first email I sent her in the summer of 2004. However, through a cosmically orchestrated synchronistic series of events over the next almost two years, my friend CW and I did establish a powerful connection with Claire. We both ended up relocating to southern Utah to work with Claire. I was hired to be Claire's business manager and CW was to be her personal assistant.

Looking back on all of this much later, I was struck by the fact of how much planning and coordination from the 'other side' occurred over long expansive periods of time for these pieces to come together. I met St. Germain in the spring of 1982. Claire met him in the Grand Tetons in 1987 and Claire and I did not meet and start working together until 2006. This was twenty-four years after my initial contact with St. Germain.

St. Germain was the catalyst, indeed!

CHAPTER 2 ,

## *The Deep Quest for Love*

We all have experienced at some time that deep, deep yearning for being loved, for being acknowledged and accepted for who we are at our core. That deep yearning has not only been the physical catalyst in our lives for finding mates, thus insuring our survival as a human species through procreation; but in a more expanded cosmic sense, it is the subconscious memory deep within our souls of being torn asunder, being separated from our "twin-flame half". We did this in order to incarnate into the plane of duality, of polarization, so we could experience the journey of separation. This deep yearning for love is not necessarily only about finding a relationship or a romantic partner, but it's the healing and gathering of all the fragmented parts of "the self" which has occurred through all lifetimes, all dimensions, and all experiences back into the state of "oneness". On the human level this yearning is the catalyst to pro-create. On the spiritual level it is the catalyst to re-member.

Twin Flames are the ripping apart and then the reintegration or reuniting of what was once whole. It is the immense power of creation. It is the power of atomic fusion and atomic destruction in the universe. We each carry this power and potential within us. Soul Mates and Twin Flame aspects when mirrored back to us through others, reveal to us our path of mastery. The more intense the Twin Flame aspects are, should we encounter them, can either trigger in us the potential for atomic fusion or atomic destruction (fission). The journey is about love of self. Twin Flames mirror back to us perfectly where we are on the journey.

If we have yet to heal our fragmented self and are more caught up in our egos and judgments, coming face-to-face with a Twin Flame aspect would most probably magnify one thousand-fold all of our unhealed wounds. In this state, often times, Twin Flame aspects who come together physically may experience such volatility it is not uncommon for them to kill each other, thinking this is the only way they could escape the intensity of that mirror. This is atomic destruction. That is part of the reason Twin Flame pairs, until now, have rarely come together at the same time, both embodied in physical incarnations.

On the other hand, when the fragmented self has been healed, made "whole again" within each person; when they, as Twin Flame aspects, come together, their union has the power of atomic fusion profoundly affecting all life way beyond their personal union.

This power of atomic fusion is profoundly illustrated by Yeshua (Jesus) and Mary Magdalene in the chapter, "In Gethsemane" from the book Anna, Grandmother of Jesus by Claire Heartsong in the following passage.

"YESHUA: For, I say to you, my Heavenly Father-Mother has established a New Covenant in me and my beloved Mary, that you now know not of but soon you shall be our witnesses. I testify that what we do shall be imprinted in you, even as the signs of crucifixion imprint my hands, wrists and feet as a testimonial that the old patterns of atoning for guilt through blood sacrifice are to be done away. So shall it be that every cell of your physical body will likewise be imprinted with the universal codes of light and truth that shall surely set you free.

ANNA: In the midst of serenading cricket song, Yeshua paused. Our attention turned to embrace the nocturnal sounds of nature around us. Then he crushed an olive leaf between his fingers and allowed the gentle breeze to send the fragments aloft. Next, my grandson picked up a nearby clod of earth, which crumbled in his hands and slowly sifted through his fingers. Smiling and acknowledging each disciple, he softly whispered, causing us to draw close to him,

YESHUA: Yea, even the least of these, which are of the Mother's earthly body, will be likewise imprinted with ascending light. No creature hidden in the deepest place will escape the irresistible pull of our cosmic Mother's love, when She brings all opposites together as divinely harmonious complements in Union. She shall surely bring down the Heavenly Father's cosmic light in order to give this earthly body a new form. We have come together at this time to assist our cosmic Mother and Father to prepare humanity and Earth for ascension's bright day, in a season yet to come.

All of you, whether physically or in your light body, were with me as I lay in the sepulcher of the Great Pyramid of Egypt. I have taken you aside and have given you additional instruction these past six years. Therefore, know that what was placed into your conscious and subconscious knowing is now being opened to you. Now you may release the Old Covenant of our matriarchal and patriarchal ancestors who believed that original sin required blood sacrifice to appease an angry, jealous god and to keep the Earth Mother fertile.

Likewise, it is you who will usher in the New Testament or New Covenant of the ascending and eternally living Christ who proclaims all life as innocent and in eternal union with its Creator. It is that same Christ living within you, who whispers this irrevocable truth to you day by day. Seek and you shall find. Knock and it shall be opened to you. It is you, my beloved companions, as you are and shall be, in a day that you now know not, who shall join with humanity to unite the highest heavenly realms of our Father with this, our beloved Earth Mother, to birth the Universal Christ into your consciousness.

If you would enter the kingdom of Heaven on Earth, allow the differences that provide contrast to inspire you. Make the two, one, by joining the inner with the outer and the outer with the inner. Allow your feelings of love to flow, giving and receiving as one. So likewise, make the upper like the lower and the lower like the upper, merging the Heavenly Father and Earthly Mother, male and female, light and darkness into a single One. In this way you shall enter the bridal chamber where the Bridegroom claims you as himself. Then you shall surely enter the kingdom." [1]

# CHAPTER 3

## ♣ *The Return to Self-Love*

Now that we've had an awareness of the Twin Flame potential of atomic destruction and atomic fusion, how do we go about healing our fragmented aspects within our own selves? This is the journey of awakening. It is the journey of first acknowledging what is there, what is in the space, and being willing to look at, work with, release and heal the wounds and faulty beliefs which are the lenses through which we choose to experience our lives. Then our awakening accelerates as we become aware and remember, at higher dimensional levels, we are "One" and still unified with our Twin Flame. Our journey of awakening means bringing that awareness and anchoring it in the living of our daily human lives here, on the earth plane, with all its challenges.

Our Twin Flame, the Beloved, is always with us and always has been with us. The Beloved is not an individual necessarily like we think of it on the earth plane, but a beingness, a vast cosmic presence. Catherine Ann shares an excerpt from her book *Soulweaving, Return*

11

*to the Heart of the Mother,* which the Magdalene Order channeled through her.

## The Magdalenes Speak through Catherine Ann

"We so love you and embrace you through this difficult time in your beingness of ALONE. It is one of the pure intense fires of alchemy; of transformation, for it is the seed that is now growing from an acorn into a mighty oak. That is who you BE. Now is the time to unravel the mystery a bit further for you will reach resolution and understanding. Keep with it just a little bit more for there is gold there, the gems of precious wisdom which you will share with others. It won't be long now. Your heartache is being relieved now for your heart has been broken for centuries, no eons really. It is a tremendous mending of many lifetimes of pain and suffering that is occurring not just for you personally, but for you collectively, as mankind in the flesh.

Mankind has suffered a broken heart for eons from the illusion of the loss of the Beloved. Now the awareness of the Beloved is returning to you. In truth, the Beloved has never left you. You have just been led to believe connecting with the Beloved is only the result of a romantic reflection; particularly if there still is a tendency to project your energy outward solely upon the "other" with the expectation that they will make you happy. The return of the Beloved is not from giving your power away, making the "other" more important than you, and having the expectation that they will fulfill your fantasy of the Beloved. No, it is the remembrance and the receiving of the

Beloved within, intimately connected to all who you are and all you have ever been; intimately breathing your breath, beating your heart, seeing through your eyes, hearing through your ears, thinking your thoughts, feeling your feelings, creating your reality, planning your life, and loving who you be and who you are being when you love others.

It is the return of the Beloved in your awareness, in your hologram within, in your realities within - and within - and within - and within - into infinity which then creates the out-picturing of the new world, what you are refer to as the 'new consciousness". It is not new. It is merely recognizing and owning the foundation and the truth of who you Be. The Beloved has always been there, has been at your side and has been deep within you, *celebrating* you. It is your Twin Flame united with you. It is the emotional body of the God within you. It is the manifestation and the expression of *Presence* in its purest, highest, most undiluted form."2

## CHAPTER 4

## ♥ *Anna Meets Her Beloved Joachim*

As we heal the fragmentation within ourselves, returning more and more to a state of wholeness, we can finally attract "another" who will be able to mirror that wholeness back to us. One of Anna's favorite stories is that of her first meeting and reunion with her Beloved in human form. Her passion for the Beloved and her joy in having the blessing of experiencing being fully met on a deep soul level exude from every word. Each word is seeded with Twin-Flame Union energy.

"ANNA: My beloved friend, I know the desire of the human heart for true love. All too often the experience of love on the earth plane is frustrated; at best a shallow reflection of that for which one secretly yearns and knows is possible. I hear your soul's prayer for a mate with whom there is rapport on all levels, especially the spiritual in which the fulfillment of your soul is to uplift life through your committed example of wholeness and unconditional love. As your soul evolves, an intense desire emerges to join your life with someone

15

with whom there can be deeply realized divine destiny.

Is such love possible? Yes, my dear friend. When all is in readiness, and most often when you least expect it, the Beloved comes forth in physical form to mirror Creator's divine love. As you come more and more into an ever-present, intimate relationship with your own eternal Beloved, as did I, you may also serve the evolution of life by attracting a soul mate with whom you perfectly mirror each other's internal mystical marriage of Divine Feminine and Masculine.

I will now share one of my most treasured memories of my experience when my beloved came into my life. As I recall, it was late in the summer season of the year 52 BC according to your calendar, when Virgo was the sign of the heavens that I was walking at dawn in the midst of the garden plot, within the cloister of the sanctuary. It was near the dormitory of the women that I paused to listen to an inner sound. This sound was as a soft, lilting trill of birdsong, and yet it was more like the sound of pipes. I wondered at its origin, for surely it was my inner ears that heard. I felt pulled by an irresistible urge to find the source of this haunting melody, which seemed to play upon the very strings of my heart. Quickly, I finished the gathering of fruits and vegetables and took them to our communal storehouse.

I kept the beckoning sounds to myself as I carefully washed the soil and sweat from my hands and face. I replaced the linens of my undergarments and to prepare my body as if for the Sabbath. My heart continued to quicken while I placed the freshest of my robes upon my slender form. As I smoothed the finely woven Egyptian cotton over my breasts and hips, I felt an unusual awareness of my body. I carefully ran my Egyptian tortoise comb through my long, thick, chestnut-brown hair, which had bleached to a flaxen color where it had been exposed to the summer sun's blistering rays. I took perfumed oil into the palms of my hands and lightly massaged it into my waist-length tresses that I plaited into a braid to be wound around my head. Because it was so unlike me to give my appearance so much attention, I wondered with increasing curiosity at that which was calling me.

With one quick glance into my polished bronze mirror, I fled out of the cloister by way of the outermost gate. Through the pastures I ran. I darted like a doe among the small groves of nut, fruit, and shade trees and the few remaining pines and cedars. Upward I climbed to the mount, my heart pounding as if to take flight from its cage within my chest. Finally, I stopped to gather myself. No one could I see, except the shepherd boys far below me, and faint hints of those who moved within the outer walls of Carmel. Seaward, there were those who were harvesting the wheat and flax upon the valley's lower hills. Warm, balmy wind currents rushed upward from the Great Sea, cooling my steamy skin and disheveling my carefully coiffed hair. All I could do was laugh at my ardent passion for the Beloved, which brought me to the top of the mount empty-handed.

I sank into the tinder-dry grasses. Tears of longing mingled with laughter's sweet release. I lay down, my back against a smooth warm stone. Soft grasses cushioned my head as I gazed into the cobalt blue sky where swallows, hawks, grackles, and sea birds darted and soared. The sun waxed overhead, and still I heard the inner music, so haunting and familiar that I was transfixed. I continued to lie there engulfed by soothing waves of bliss, fed with effulgent nectar. Slowly, I dissolved in an ocean of flame. Such burning! I was too drunk to stand.

So the hours passed until I finally began to come to myself, still not knowing the purpose of my spontaneous excursion or the source of the heartfelt sound. When once I was able to rise to my feet, smoothing my skirts about me, I thought to myself, "I must gather herbs, roots, and flowers. There must be some explanation for my going." So I began to pluck stems, leaves, berries, rosehips, and petals. Roots I dug, until my outer skirt and shawl could hold no more. Then, there were wild roses and a handful of summer lilies which, last of all, were picked to place upon the altar.

I was so engaged in my labors that I did not notice when the inner song became the same as the song that wafted upon the breeze. It was only when I stood up, my cornucopia harvest gathered, that I realized the lovely sounds I heard were coming from across the crest of the hill beyond me. Carefully, I carried my treasure to the precipice and knelt amidst the boulders. Not far below, beneath the shade of a lonely cedar, was a robed minstrel. In turn, he played the lyre and pipes. So this was the music that had played upon my very heart, calling me to the mount. I gazed unashamed while drinking in the melodies he sang and played. Then, as if sensing me, he turned his tanned, bearded face to scan the ridge above him. Our eyes locked in an eternal embrace.

Such joy! Here, at last, in physical form was the one I knew mirrored my soul in perfect wholeness! An unquenchable burning arose from somewhere deep within me to consume any remaining resistance that I might have to fully dissolving into the vast arms of the Beloved on High. While fully aware of every sensation throbbing throughout my body, my soul again took free flight.

As if attracted by a magnet so strong that nothing could keep us apart, I let go of my precious harvest, except for my handful of the season's last roses and lilies, and ran to the path that led to the lone, ancient cedar below. Before I rounded the last outcrop of boulders, there he was running toward me. Catching ourselves just in time, we slowed to a measured gait, each eyeing the other, weighing feeling against reason, as we approached our moment of truth. Tears welled up from the tension of holding within our breasts eons of longing for the Beloved incarnate. Our eyes blazed with light. Out of our lips passed a suppressed sigh. Then, peals of laughter, quickened with deep recognition, lightened our steps until we stood before one another, face to face. I thrust the bouquet into his hand and, like a deer, almost bolted away, but he reached out and took me into his arms. Gently, he cupped my face, and stroked my cheeks, flushed and glistening with tears.

I hardly knew what to do with myself, feeling awkward and shy. Not knowing what to say, I silently allowed myself to be with this man, who announced that he was known as Heli to his Persian brothers and Joachim to his brothers of Galilee. The sun haloed his face. His curled, salt and pepper hair spun tendrils of midnight blue and silver. In that moment, he was a Greek sun god. It was as if Helios stood before me. For me, Joachim would never do. At that moment, in my heart, he became Heliochim. After I introduced him, the Carmel community began to call him Joachim, as I came to do.

My beloved towered above me, my head abreast of his heart. His shoulders were wide, his bearing strong. Lean was his form, contouring the bleached linen robe he wore. His long, densely tangled hair denoted a Nazarite Jew, a group of ascetic Essenes who wandered the lands much as the saddhus of India live by the Mother's grace. His hair was parted in the middle, as worn by those of Galilee, yet his olive complexioned skin and dark, almond-shaped, oriental eyes told me he was also Persian.

As we stood looking upon one another, reading our energy fields, I remembered the moment, several months ago, when I was lifted into the light realms with Isis and Osiris. My vision returned as I beheld before me the one who had knelt at the feet of the Christed master, Maitreya. Then, I knew who he was and realized that now was the time to bring the covenant of our one soul to fruition. At last when I could catch my breath, my winged heart content to rest, I introduced myself.

I noticed my voice, softer and lower in pitch than usual, as I explained who I was and my station at Carmel. As if catching up on a very long history, like children reciting our lessons, we informed one another's inquisitive minds, while all the time feeling the undeniable testimony of our hearts singing familiar, ancient rhythms. Our hands could not leave the other's clasp until we noticed the rays of the sun had passed behind the mount. The sound of a bell reverberated its call to the faithful to come to evening prayers and the communal supper table. Responsibility and a childlike eagerness to share the excitement of Joachim's arrival with my Carmel family moved us to gather our things we had laid aside during our rendezvous hour.

Down the uppermost slopes of Mount Carmel we descended, in joyful anticipation of Joachim's first meeting with Joseph and Martha. Those gathering around the long tables would soon see us washed and prepared for Joachim's formal introduction. So it was that my beloved and I entered the outer gate to bring our lives and destiny together within Carmel's sanctuary of peace."[3]

CHAPTER 5

# ♥ *The Nature of Twin Flame Relationships*

"ANNA: Now that I have shared my story about my meeting with Joachim, who was my soul mate as well as my twin-soul and twin-flame, I will briefly explain the nature of soul mate relationships, a very popular and misunderstood topic. Every soul has numerous soul mates, both physical and spiritual. You might think of soul mates as a huge extended family that lives on the earth plane and also in the realms of light. However, before external relationships with soul mates can be understood, it is vital to become intimate with your internal soul with whom there is an eternal bonding.

Although I will elaborate on external relationships, I wish to emphasize the importance of establishing a loving and accepting relationship with your self – your physical, emotional, mental, and spiritual aspects integrated into a wholeness of being.

Some individuals mistakenly put their lives "on hold" thinking they can only do their divine purpose with a spiritual partner. Some miss their appropriate soul mate because they cannot accept the human element that disguises the soul essence of their beloved. If you find yourself single, or with a partner, who is either spiritually asleep or awake, please know that your primary and most fulfilling soul mate relationship is with your beloved Self." [4]

## Chapter 6

# The Lonely Path of the Lightworker

*(The following material is Anna's response to a question about soulmate relationships asked by Martine Vallee, editor and publisher at Ariane Editions, Montreal, Canada who has translated and published both "Anna, Grandmother of Jesus" and "Anna, the Voice of the Magdalenes" into French making them available in all French speaking countries.")*

MARTINE: (The lonely path of the Light worker): *As a publisher, I often receive phone calls or letters from my readership and one thing that always comes back to me is how many lightworkers feel lonely and can't seem to find a companion with the same spiritual purpose. It is as if we are in different corridors, never able to join together. I was told that the year 2010 will be the end of the loneliness that many feel because of an outpouring of light which has as its main purpose to reunite the sacred feminine and sacred masculine together. I have also been told that we could expect 2010 to be a year of complementary companionship, one in which we are joined by new energies and acquaintances. Since this book will be published in August 2010, would you agree with this statement?*

*Would have anything to add to help those who wish to be reunited with their soul mate or spiritual partners?*

ANNA: The question I would pose to my beloved lightworkers, who are feeling lonely and bereft of kindred companions and intimate soulmates with whom to share your journey, is, "Are you the kind of companion and intimate soulmate you wish to attract into your embrace?" If you find that you are, then you have only to open your arms. If not, then you are now more aware of what you put between you and what you desire –some form of fear – perhaps a fearful story you continue telling yourself in order to feel safe.

I would suggest that you also ask yourself these questions, "Am I truly ready to know myself in the Divine Mirror?" "Am I willing to suffer the grief that comes when my projected ideal self – "my beloved," crumbles and dies? Can I celebrate the possibility of truly seeing and knowing my beloved sitting across from me without projected filters and expectations?" "Am I willing and ready to commit to being fully present for my beloved – my heart open when I want to close it? Can I be present as both beloved and the Beloved over the "long haul?"

If so, then: "Am I willing to embrace and heal the opposite polarity of love in myself that my soulmate reflects and so precisely triggers into my awareness?" "Am I willing to bring love and mercy to my beloved as I embrace his or her suffering as my own?" "Am I open and vulnerable to the healing love my beloved gives to me?" "Can I rejoice in my beloved's happiness?" "Can I celebrate and faithfully enter into the amplified intensity of our joined soulmate karmas as we forgive and transmute them in the alchemical fires of divine love?"

24

If you answer, "Yes!" to most of these questions, then you cannot stop your beloved soulmate(s) from coming to you. You will also enjoy the companionship of kindred souls – like attracts like, when we make ourselves available. We are family joining together, supporting one another and bringing greater benefit to all life. Through the synergy of, "Where two or more are gathered in a unity of purpose…," we can accomplish anything.

All these questions lead us to the popular topic of soul mates. Because there is so much interest, I wish now to speak about the various stages or levels of initiation involved in conscious *soulmate relationships*, which can lead the soul out of the prison of duality. It is important to remember that it is this deep yearning for union and liberation that, ultimately, is the reason for so much interest – it's not just about getting more and better romantic love.

In order to understand my point of view, which may assist you in attaining the ultimate purpose of soulmate relationships; it is important to establish a context or container wherein we can view the various levels. First of all, as long as the initiate is unenlightened and is in a physical body, there will be elements or qualities of consciousness which inter-penetrate all the levels, more or less, depending on how conscious or unconscious he or she is. Unconscious relationships express a greater degree of duality consciousness. Conscious relationships are based in unity consciousness. As the initiate awakens to unity consciousness, there are benchmarks which distinguish his or her progress.

Unawakened men and women relate to each other in dualistic and survival-based ways – "I and other" or "I versus other." Most of the relational experiences within unconscious relationships are habituated, conditioned, reactive and competitive. Most human beings on planet Earth, at this time, are experiencing the suffering that naturally comes with perceived separation and identification with the physical body – the first relationship level.

As the innate self-liberating, compassionate essence of the soul rises into increasing awareness, the awakening initiate crosses a pivotal threshold. There is an opening of the heart to unconditional love. Perceived "other" is seen in an entirely new way – not as someone entirely distinct from self; but as a fellow brother or sister who is equally deserving of happiness. Relating to other means more "I and thou" and "I am you." Now there is more possibility for greater harmony and deep healing. Deeply conditioned dualistic minds are now observed with greater clarity and compassion.

When the heart opens there is a yearning to be with kindred souls whose hearts are also opening. There is a deep mutual desire for conscious experiences of true intimacy and union. Happiness is chosen over being right. Harmony and peaceful co-existence is more the norm than the ceaseless suffering that comes when unconscious hearts are defensive and closed.

## Soul Mates as Divine Complements

ANNA: The dynamic of opposites or complementary polarities attracting one another are usually experienced within the early stages of conscious soulmate relationships. *Divine complements* come together to reflect what is judged, abandoned and rejected – unconscious obscurations - within self, for the purpose of healing karmas and opening the heart further to infinite compassion and to Divine Love – the Beloved.

Masculine and feminine energies are explored and their balanced union is brought into awareness. This level may be explored over many lifetimes.

At this level you may find yourself with a soulmate who seems to be "not on the path." Or you may find yourself with partners who come and go in rapid succession. Or you may be single for years or possibly your entire life – relating to your soulmate through the ethers or over the Internet. Or you are experiencing a lifetime spouse who harmoniously complements you, with whom you share mutual devotion and the same spiritual path – you do not rock each other's boat. In this lifetime you have come together to rest and to develop skills for more intense experiences of mastery later." [5]

## CHAPTER 7

## ♥ *Soul Mates/Twin Souls/Twin Flame Alchemy*

What are the different alchemical dynamics and levels of consciousness involved in Soul Mate, Twin Soul and Twin Flame relationships?

### Soul Mates as Divine Mirrors

"ANNA: Soul mates, like divine complementary mirrors, perfectly reflect your consciousness in every moment. Sometimes the reflection may express as the opposite polarity from the one that you are consciously experiencing, but what you perceive is still mirroring your energy, which is expressing through the same resonance. You attract these experiences so that both of you can be conscious of your subconscious and shadow material. Then you have the opportunity to harmonize and balance the polarities within self as well as those that emerge within the chemistry of your combined relationship.

Soul mates are not limited to sexually intimate relationships.

They can be relatives, teachers, friends, and even enemies. Always, they come into your life and you into theirs, at the perfect time when your soul desires accelerated growth and healing of separation consciousness. Because there is so much love between you on a soul level, your souls agree before you incarnate that you will find one another and that you will play the most appropriate roles in your life's dramas.

These relationships prepare each of you for your highest empowerment and destiny. Sometimes those roles are very loving and harmonious. Sometimes there can be extreme suffering. Nevertheless, the ultimate purpose of soul mate relationships is to enter into a divine relationship in which the self is at first mirrored. Then once clarified through forgiveness and compassionate love, the Beloved who has always been present is revealed. Through self-knowledge and self-empowerment gained in conscious relationship, each soul remembers how to be present for both self and the perceived other.

The giving and receiving of love through all kinds of relationships becomes the greatest of eternally expanding gifts. One way or the other, your soul comes to understand there are no victims, no tyrants, and truly there is nothing to forgive. Yet, forgiveness is the key that opens a wounded and callused heart to feeling the love that it has been missing and craving. Forgiving, compassionate love sees self and others in innocence. This love without limits is the open door that brings Heaven to Earth."[6]

## Twin Souls as Divine Mirrors of Oneness: Reflections of Divinity

"ANNA: This stage, the stage of divine complements may

overlap with the beginning stages of the next level – twin souls.

For those who have opened their hearts more fully to Divine Love through the embrace of opposites and are ready to progress further, the dynamic of twin-souls may be experienced. Now the couple experiences "twin-ness" in the Divine Mirror. There is the synergy of likes coming together – the same karmic strengths and weaknesses, which are now greatly amplified. This dynamic facilitates deeper levels of alchemy, union and spiritual mastery on all levels. All this prepares the devoted twin-soul couple to the great letting go of the separate self.

With twin-souls there is a mutual awareness of and alignment with the Beloved. The Beloved – the true Self beyond the conceptual mind, is consciously invited to be an integral, triangulated aspect of this path of spiritual awakening. Twin-soul couples intentionally choose a relational spiritual path that includes conscious sexuality with or without physical penetration rather than a spiritual path that involves strict celibacy without a sexual partner.

The completion stages of the twin-soul level overlap with the next evolving spiral.

In the more expanded levels of conscious relationship there is a deeply profound commitment to using conscious relationship as a spiritual path which leads to being fully awakened for the sake of all beings. Twin souls or spiritual consorts now endeavor to become the embodied Beloved.

## CHAPTER 8

## ♥ *Twin Flame Union*

The culminating stage of this level of conscious relationship is that these transmuted and awakened twin souls now prepare themselves for the ultimate inter-dimensional and cosmic union – what I call *Twin-Flame Union*. Merging in this way cannot be grasped by ordinary consciousness. Very few beings choose to undertake these very intense initiations. However, there are increasing numbers of couples on this demanding and noble path. When you are ready, I shall meet you there!"[7]

### Remembered Wholeness

Wholeness attracts wholeness. You are here on this earth plane to accelerate your soul's evolution into that Wholeness and to be of service so that you can eventually match the cosmic frequency of your Twin Flame.

Along the journey into remembered wholeness you will have

many soul mates who come to you from your soul groupings to assist you as divine mirrors reflecting back to you how you are experiencing yourself. Are you whole? Or are you reacting to a perceived lack of missing parts, or judging the parts you have as unworthy of love? As a catalyst, your soul mate assists you to be whole and balanced with your masculine and feminine energies. This process brings increasing capacity for embodying the frequencies of your Twin Flame. Soul mates assist you through the purification process so that you can say "Yes!" to more Divine Love. They assist you to be one with your Beloved I AM and Christ Presence so that you can have a unified perspective and can choose to move beyond dualistic dramas into the unity that is Twin Flame.

As the perceived distinctions of "self" and "other" - "twin-ness" - alchemically burn and dissolve in the union of the two flames made One, the veil of duality is lifted. Experiencing liberation from the prison of separation and stepping into the absolute clear light of Oneness, the true face of the Beloved is recognized - the union of blissful, omniscient awareness and pure, unborn and undying radiance. This is the ultimate realization of Twin-Flame Union.

# CHAPTER 9

## ♥ *Divine Sexual Expression*

"ANNA: I could go on and on about the empowerment that comes through conscious, sacred relationship with the whole of life, which by the way, is constantly immersed in the free-flow of divine sexual expression. Indeed, I have come to celebrate all life as sexual! Human sexuality, when it is consciously and compassionately expressed through an awakened heart, becomes a powerful spiritual path in which you may come to know your Self as the Love, Lover, and the Beloved. Although this terrain of the heart – so often misunderstood – is near and dear to me, I will bring my discussion to a close. Meanwhile, let us turn inward and feel the gentle presence of the Beloved with whom you are already eternally wed."[8]

CLAIRE: Indeed, much could be said about the topic of sexuality which is on everyone›s minds. However, you will only rarely find the subject of divine sexuality and conscious relationship, as a path of spiritual awakening, considered, much less practiced.

Although much could be shared about sexuality's very

35

important dynamic energy and the alchemical, tantric practices that may be cultivated in soulmate, twin soul and twin flame relationships, I am choosing to say very little. Instead, I encourage you to call forth and deeply contemplate authentic teachers, teachings and practices that are sufficiently empowered to take you all the way home into Union.

You will easily find Westernized tantric practices in the local bookstore or online; but these are usually a more expanded way to disguise dualistic human sexuality. These practices may provide some degree of opening and maturation, but they usually lead to dead ends. They can be a step in the right direction, but these superficial practices and their adherents cannot take you to your ultimate destination.

It is important to know that traversing the terrain of subtle energy currents and participating in other profound Tantric/ alchemical practices that transmute conditioned karmic patterns is dangerous on many levels. You may have gathered the wisdom, merit and remembrance of these practices from former lives in order to accomplish the journey alone; but it is wise to be humble and teachable so that a teacher(s) who has realized more than you have can serve as your guide(s). There are realized tantric masters living on the earthplane. There are authentic teachings and practices based on harmlessness and unity consciousness. May all obstacles be removed so that you may attract authentic guides into your life, if you so choose. As the adage goes, "When the student is ready, the teacher appears."

May your deepest heart's longing for enlightenment and Twin Flame Union be fulfilled in this lifetime. May it be so for yourself and all beings!

## Chapter 10

## ♥ *Healing Separation Consciousness*

Embodying the Divine Feminine allows the possibility of embracing and coming into union with all that we perceive as "other" than self, thus healing separation consciousness. The nature of Twin Flame Union is the merged embrace of perceived opposites.

"ANNA: Preparing to meet and merge with your Twin Flame will stir the pot grandly. It will bring out the most blatant expressions of polarity within self. So it is not the Hollywood romance you may be attached to by any means. For it is to understand that Twin Flame Union playing out in duality consciousness is one of meeting and merging with opposite and complementary expressions of energy.

You have chosen this manner of knowing yourself so that you may return to an awareness of unity in which you can love without condition. What you call the Divine Mother is the ultimate expression of all-embracing love. So it is that when you align with the Divine Mother you can embrace all the parts of you that your separated consciousness most avoids and judges. You bring these aspects into

37

the Heart of Love. Your eyes become the Eye that sees only original purity and innocence. You recognize that you are the Light that dissolves the obscuring darkness of ignorance - the Heart that enfolds the All without condition.

And this, beloveds, is why it is vital to welcome the return of the Divine Feminine and to allow the Divine Mother to express through you. As you do this you are simultaneously bringing yourself to your Twin Flame and your Twin Flame to you. Your journey may bring forth your Twin Flame as a soul mate or a twin-soul, but don't wait around for an ideal lover or immediately reject a soul mate who comes unto you because he or she doesn't meet your expectations or rubs you the wrong way.

Does this assist you beloveds? Any questions about what I have shared? Disappointments, or is this a relief?

CW: No. I think everyone is looking for an explanation and that feels very comfortable. I appreciate it. It's a very much higher ideal than most would consider. Most people are running around frantically looking for their Twin Flame. I think the higher our frequency gets, the more love we become and the more we are able to sense the presence of our Twin Flame...

ANNA: Absolutely! And you know, beloveds, you are then able to be with anyone of humanity and know that that one, no matter how they are expressing themselves, is also your Twin Flame – your Beloved. As Mother Teresa held the beggar dying in her arms, she knew this suffering soul was her beloved Christ. From a more expanded understanding she was able to feel her Twin Flame energy expressing as the one lying in her arms. Within the core of her heart she was intent on knowing Twin Flame love absolutely in that embrace and she brought that individual home into that knowing of love also.

Do you know who Mother Teresa's embodied opposite twin flame energy was in the scenario of that lifetime, even though on the surface this may seem contrary to what I was just sharing? You would not think such an individual could hold any measure of the frequency I am talking about, but in the understanding of opposite mirrors, in third dimensional duality, the opposite twin-flame energy expressing in physicality was (an infamous tyrant). So sometimes you don't want to know who your embodied twin flame is because it could be your polar opposite – especially if you, as Mother Theresa, are choosing to be very polarized on the "light" side of the coin.

CA: Yeah, then your twin flame would be polarized in the opposite ...

ANNA: Yes, that is correct in the understanding of complementary polarities perceived as irreconcilable opposites. Mother Teresa›s soul and mindstream evolved and matured greatly through her choice to serve and hold the suffering of the "untouchables" as though they were her beloved Christ. Holding the suffering masses of Calcutta to her deepest heart was Mother Teresa's way of touching and beginning to embrace the "hidden untouchable" parts of her consciousness in that lifetime.

You, like Mother Teresa, are on the ascending journey of what I call Twin Flame Union where you will eventually embody your Twin Flame at a cosmic level. As you move more and more into a unified understanding that is beyond dualism, you realize that both polarities are within yourself. Then you do not psychically split and fragment and require the opposite mirror any longer.

At that stage when you really know that you don't need another to complete you, nor are you avoiding the other who reflects what you used to judge as unlovable, it is then in a moment of non-expectancy that your Twin on the other side of the veil will pop into apparency.

At that point, you will be sufficiently prepared to embrace the intense magnification of energies coming home to roost in the innermost center of your heart. You will be able recognize and behold the true face of your Beloved as your own in form and beyond form simultaneously.

## CHAPTER 11

## ♥ *Cosmic Twin Flame Union*

Whether we are aware, or not, of subtle levels of consciousness, we are none-the-less experiencing the dying/birthing process that accompanies cosmic Twin Flame Union. If we pause to reflect and witness, we can feel the intensifying alchemical pressure and terrifying stretching that is transmuting us and our world reality as we have known it. Within and without, we are feeling the effects of the imploding and exploding energies that are expressing on a planetary level.

We are immersed in increasing chaos because we, as a collective global humanity, are integrally and inseparably connected with what Mother Earth is experiencing. We are her body; and her body is dying from the exponential and harmful effects of our collective separation consciousness. We are also her intrinsic, expanded consciousness choosing Twin Flame Union. As a result, we, as Mother Earth, are giving birth to a greater harmonic expression of unity and freedom. As we have greater awareness of Twin Flame

Union's birthing/dying process, we can meet each personal and global contraction and expansion with greater calm and with skillful mastery and compassionate presence. It is a matter of choice between love and fear as polarization becomes more extreme.

The energies of inevitable change are gathering into a critical mass. We are being forced to awaken from our conditioned fear-based denial of impermanence, uncertainty and death. At first we are like deer standing paralyzed in a car's headlights. We are shocked by the dying and loss that is glaringly apparent all around us. If we have not stabilized ourselves in love and gratitude, we will automatically react and go into survival mode, focusing on what we most fear. We either run around frantically trying to distract ourselves, filling every moment with busyness, courting death by taking high risks. Or we sink into a lethargic, dull stupor and disconnect from life by slowly dying into some form of immobilizing depression.

Caught in our mind's dark imaginings, lost in past and future, we lose awareness of the present moment in which we are birthing something new and vibrantly alive. We ignore Mother Earth's invitation to come to her "birthday party." A party in which we may come together and dance ourselves awake with clear awareness; an exhilarating party where the birthing process is celebrated rather than feared and lamented; a party where we can join together in a heart-opening, unifying sphere of Oneness.

Humanity stands at a pivotal point. We can embrace our separation fears and join our Mother, the Earth, as she merges with her Twin Flame energy. We can generate the courage and skills needed to ride the cosmic waves of Twin Flame Union that have the potential to lift us into ultimate freedom and union. We can choose to be present in the now - the only time there is. We can choose to relax our grip on our identification with duality and our self-clinging addictions. Or we can choose to succumb to fear's crushing waves and anger's explosive fragmentation. We can choose to take advantage of the freedoms and opportunities we now have in this precious human body to awaken and be free. Or we can be recycled again and again for countless eons hoping for another opportunity in some distant future.

We can relax and smile at fear. Like the great liberator, St. Germain, we can bring levity to our human predicament and remember:

## "FREEDOM is spelled R - E - L - A - X!"

As we relax and allow all our fragmented aspects to merge in our expanded awareness, we come to know that we are inseparably connected with our Twin Flame - our Beloved I AM. Our hearts and minds are opened and we are purified of the obscurations that we have accumulated over innumerable lifetimes. With greater clarity and compassion, we begin to realize that everyone and everything perceived as external objects - even our internal witnessing awareness - are not separate entities.

As dualistic perception is cleansed and healed, all that is perceived through our senses and imagination becomes increasingly like a play of pure light, sound and color. We realize that what we took to be our reality is a mirage-like projection created by the magical power our own minds. Calmly resting with our breath, we realize that within this movement there is the calm abiding of inseparable stillness and bliss. And within this stillness, unconditional love automatically arises for all beings. Having compassion for our own suffering, we also have compassion for everyone who suffers the consequences of ignorantly choosing to be separate from the unnamable Oneness that is the truth of our being. The journey into Twin Flame Union returns us to that Oneness. Rejoicing in the increasing freedom from suffering that naturally arises; we have a desire to bring that same freedom, harmony, peace and well-being to our families, communities, nations and our beloved planet"[9]

# CHAPTER 12

## ♥ *Twin Flames in Service to Humanity*

The conscious drawing together of Twin Flames serves not only the Twin Flame pair, but serves humanity from the perspective of simultaneously being humanity's Twin Flame as well. Anna invites us to join her in the embracing arms of the cosmic Twin Flame energies that are bringing us Home; sharing her vision of serving humanity from the perspective of seeing and being "both flames" simultaneously in Union. As the merging occurs, dualistic boundaries and distinctions dissolve into the embracing arms of cosmic Twin Flame energies. The following is a portion of the transcription of a "2006 Anna Fireside Chat" with three friends, including Catherine Ann.

"ANNA: When Twin Flame energies come together in a conscious way in order to bring about enormous benefit for all humanity - all beings - animate and inanimate, indeed, the entire planet and omni-universe, there is a generation and magnification of energy as it comes into alchemical union. A critical mass is generated similar to the point just before a star dies into supernova and then births new stars, galaxies and universes. A broad spectrum of light frequencies goes out as cosmic waves inter-penetrating space and all particles within it. Some of these frequencies are of a higher, more harmonious expression of light, sound and color. The more that you can tune into and embody these higher frequencies the easier it will be for you to pass through the dying/birthing process of cosmic Twin Flame Union.

The earth and humanity have crossed enough of the dissonant thresholds to begin to tip the scales. It only requires a relatively few who are matching their frequencies with that of their Twin Flame consciousness to create a critical mass. It's very much like untwisting a spindle and bringing what's in – OUT, untying the binding knots of separation and status quo, as it were. Allowing what is passing away to gracefully leave our grasp, while welcoming what is emerging from the void – the Source of All that Is.

CA: And so the more we are able to step into that and hold the space communally, it not only raises the frequency but it draws the people who are ready to also remember and be activated by the hologram frequency of Twin Flame Union that is already seeded in their DNA.

ANNA: Exactly.

CA: The magnetism is there.

ANNA: Let's look at a possible scenario that might cause you to feel angry or fearful. What if you were to get all up in arms with your President's decisions to do this and that and another? What if you were to get involved in a fearful way with all the people involved with the conspiracy movement or religious fundamentalism? And you were writing to your congressmen and you were writing to all of your peers through the Internet and you were saying you've got to get busy and you've got to take action against this particular thing that is happening. What would be the result of that action if you were angry and fearful, even if it were justified?

JH: You'd increase what you fear or are angry about, so to speak.

ANNA: Indeed. And taking that kind of action, because you are in fear, you'd be pushing your ascended Twin Flame energy away.

CW: Your frequency drops and your Twin Flame cannot meet you in fear.

ANNA: Exactly.

CW: It's a terribly agitated way to be.

ANNA: Exactly. Does that mean that you do not do something about the situations that are impeding liberty and justice and freedom?

CW: It's about what is in your heart and what you think and how you are going about it.

ANNA: As individuals begin to embody, transmute and harmonize both polarities within themselves they can create a harmonizing ripple effect wherever they are, whether it's in Congress, the White House or on the battlefield. Just one person who is empowered with Twin Flame energy can work miracles and can change entrenched laws that impede freedom. When you know that war and conflict in the world and in your families is a reflection of your own inner battle, you can pause and find resolution first within self; then the outer reflection will begin to change – sometimes without even actively doing anything to change it. There's a peace and calm that comes and an ability to respond in appropriate ways instead of reacting in a knee-jerk fashion. There is wisdom, there is compassion and there is also an ability to step up, take a stand and do what is required at the time.

What I am saying does not mean to have no personal boundaries or to avoid taking appropriate action in a timely fashion when it's necessary. I am inviting you to be discerning and skillful as you embrace all the energy that comes onto you. Ultimately all this energy that is expressing is a gift of yourself to yourself so that you can know and love yourself more fully. Ultimately it is your Twin Flame energy coming unto you to embrace and merge with you. And it is you as Twin Flame come forth in vulnerability and clarity of perception to merge in union with the entirety of you.

Once you claim the gift of self-awareness and choice, you don't have to simply put up with or join in with the dramatization of afflictive emotions and conflicted conditions, unless you choose to have these reflections. The projections in the mirror do provide you with opportunities for self-mastery and relieving others' suffering. At some point you will grow tired of all the recycled melodrama and you will be sufficiently motivated to fold up the stage and close the theatre.

It is to be wise and gentle with yourself while you are going through the process of learning how to transmute the toxic and discordant energy that keeps the soap opera, "As the World Turns" revolving through your mind and relationships. Do not hesitate to say "No!" when something or someone's presence is harmful or is lowering your frequency. Do not give your power away to an authority outside yourself, even if it's coming from an ascended consciousness like mine. At some point you will know you are the Magician and the magic show. So am I, and I am you! We are playing charades and peek-a- boo for the fun of it! Are we having fun yet? Freedom – Union – Nowness! F-U-N!

My approach to sovereignty and union is a pragmatic course

that encourages prosperity of health and wealth on this earth plane. If your ascension process is not increasing your mastery on the physical plane right down to the cellular level and helping you to be happy and content with what you have - and I am not talking about quantity, but quality of life - having gratitude and appreciation for every breath and every being and everything that comes unto you, then it will not take you all the way. That is, you will not know how to be the full spectrum of energy that is involved in Twin Flame Union.

It's not necessary to dramatize your internal discord in order to transmute it. In fact, that is one way to keep the drama going. Instead of projecting it outward, there is much that you can do internally to harmonize mental, emotional and physical discord in your meditations, in your healing sessions and in your dream time. However, I suggest a word to the wise when you approach people or situations as a healer - playing "savior." If you go in with an invalidating judgment in which you think there is something to fix or to rescue, you will most likely feed into and unconsciously keep the discord going so that you can maintain your ego identity as a healer/rescuer/victim - perhaps even pretending to be a "Twin Flame" - not knowing what that really means.

Allow everyone to have the experiences they are choosing, for they are gaining wisdom, as are you. Instead, consider the power of your pacifying example and issue an invitation to others to consider the possibility of choosing a more expanded option – perhaps share what you find is working for you. Then let it be without attaching to expectation or outcome. Be the Light and show the way with an attitude of latitude. Be happy. Laugh heartily. Laughter is the great aligner of discord!

It is time for us to stand impeccably in a place of balance and harmony knowing we are truly expressions of love. It's easier said than done when all kinds of chaos reigns, but you have lots of assistance. Standing together we can accomplish more than we ever have in Earth's long history. So, my beloveds, remember your cosmic Mother's love and your Twin Flame's empowering presence that you have touched, and that touched you, this evening. May this always be a comfort to you as you remember and choose Twin Flame Union for the benefit of all beings - for all beings are You - your Twin-Flame!"[10]

# CHAPTER 13

## ♣ *The Magdalenes and Twin Flame Union*

The Magdalene Order is dedicated to the resurrection of consciousness throughout all time and all ages. Its purpose is to prepare consciousness on all levels for Twin Flame Union. Many of us today, both women and men, have had previous lives in the ancient Order of Isis and in other temples, orders, and cultural groups which are part of the Magdalene Order. Even though in our conscious minds we may not be aware of this, deep within our subconscious mind and deep within our souls we know we are here to be of service. We are here to uphold the light and the resurrection of consciousness to awaken into a new consciousness which will prepare for union with our Twin Flame. We are awakening to our path of service, awakening to the awareness we are of the Magdalene Order, returned to this earth plane once again, to continue our journey of awakening and helping others to awaken.

Many of us feel we have a message to share. We are not only evolving through our individual journey back to Twin Flame Union, but we sense there now larger communal support available to us both within and externally, as we walk this path of re-membering.

## ♥ Anna Speaks About the Magdalenes

"ANNA: *(Addressing a woman who shared that she wanted to know more about Mary Magdalene and how to bring her own work out which she felt she'd been being prepared to do for a long time.)* Perhaps more than ever it is a time for communal support and teaching and sharing what you have been learning. Then the memories will come back of what you knew in your mastery during the time of Yeshua. Get out and do it beloved, share it, write about it and allow your light to shine. Know that you are not alone. You are not alone. And you will be heard.

Much of what is occurring now is the opening and freeing up of the voice of the feminine to express in both men and women. The suppressed feminine aspect, especially her silenced voice, is rising in consciousness. Humanity stands collectively at the threshold of a huge opening of the throat and the throat chakra energies to create a new reality of equality, equanimity and balanced harmony. The bell (the feminine) of liberty and freedom shall be rung and heard around the world. The secret deeds of tyrannical despots will have no place to hide, the earth-raping and power mongering agendas of governments and corporations will be brought out of the shadows. Patriarchal dominance will stand exposed in its impotence. You are in the midst of great change. You are the voice of empowered change - change wrought through balanced masculine and feminine expression.

So I say to you, you shall be heard! First of all hear yourself – hear the parts of you that have been silently screaming, that feel unheard; the parts of you that are angry at you, your parents, your lover or the system, or whatever is perceived as preventing you from fully creating the beauty, majesty, fullness and wholeness of who you really are. If you wish, come together in community and co-create a supportive container for one another's collective anger. Skillfully create a container that is large enough to hold all your stories - "If only this person had done, or not done, such and such to me, or if I had not done such and such...." - all the blame and victim stories and dramas that you know so well. Write these stories down. Express them through music, art and dance and theatrical performance instead of the battlefield. Create healing spaces with your brothers and sisters so that your stories can safely, lovingly, compassionately, and honestly be expressed until peaceful resolutions comes.

At some point the disillusion and weariness with the endlessly recycled stories about gain and loss, hope and fear will be sufficient to motivate finding a way out of the conditioned mind's prison. You can begin to embrace your suffering as being no different than everyone else's. A great compassion arises and a fervent desire to liberate yourself and others.

In this way you can begin to see all your stories with new eyes - speak your stories with open throats and listen to your voices with open ears - begin to embrace all your story/creation with an open feminine heart, the heart of the Divine Mother - the heart of the Magdalene.

WOMAN: What does that mean? What do you mean when you say the heart of the Magdalene?

ANNA: Let me first of all say that to understand what the term «the heart of the Magdalene» means is to know that there was not just one Magdalene, the Mary Magdalene you have been told about, but there have been and still are many Magdalenes. The Magdalenes are comprised of both men and women. The majority of Magdalenes through history have been women because the Magdalene orientation is basically the all-embracing feminine mode of being. Since this long era has favored the masculine analytical, discriminating view with an emphasis on doing, few men are able to align with the Magdalenes. They are not aligned with and distrust the feminine within themselves - and consequently they distrust the women who are Magdalenes.

Originally, in very ancient times, the Magdalenes were an offshoot, a tributary of the mysteries of Isis which involved the Osirian resurrection processes. So it was that the Magdalenes, as they came to be known in ancient Israel, were originally trained in the alchemies of Isis in Egypt. Their specialty was and is to resurrect consciousness from its perceived separation or dualistic state.

The initiated Magdalenes all share a willingness to bring great benefit to a suffering humanity because they are motivated by love and compassion. They share confidence in the process because they have acquired the necessary skills from those who know how to descend into the abyss, into the hell realms, into the shit - the compost, as I prefer to call all the accumulated karmic suffering of humanity throughout time. We may hold up our skirts a bit, but nevertheless, we get down in it with immense love. We stomp the grapes (ego-clinging), extract the juice (pure, intrinsic essence), and make wine (ascended/ enlightened consciousness). The first requirement is recognizing that the "compost" is pure, pristine energy in its essential nature. Then, however it presents itself, it is accepted for what it is and allowed to just be.

Enfolding all manner of separation consciousness with our all-encompassing heart's wings (the Great Mother Isis' wings) - the

Magdalene heart becomes an infallible alchemical container - a heart/ womb grail - into which the full-spectrum of polarized ingredients can come together. Within the container there is plenty of space for the "dark" and "light" energies to court one another, penetrate one another and come into a cosmic fusion when sufficient heat is generated. The energy is no longer darkness nor is it light; but rather an aura of golden brilliance. A radiant form of clear rainbow light comes forth from the grail womb and is recognized as the beloved Christ/ Osiris resurrected from the death state of separation. The realized or enlightened Magdalenes are those who know the resurrecting path of 'the Beloved' - the way of Twin Flame Union.

Another term for Magdalene is watchtower. We are like a watch tower with an omniscient view - a 360 degree, omni-dimensional, omni-directional point of view. In the alchemical story of Isis and Osiris, Osiris was killed by his jealous brother and his body was scattered by the winds across the face of the earth. From her watchtower, Isis looked and then went out and gathered all the fragments of her beloved and brought them into union in the innermost, indestructible center of her heart. This was not just a reuniting of Osiris' body parts; but a Union of Twin Flames in which she herself merged fully with her Beloved. As sun and moon melded and fused together in union they birthed a new creation, Horus - the Son/Sun beyond the sun.

It is important to understand your resurrecting, ascending process is not limited by gender – Magdalenes are not gender specific. Remember this truth: men embody the liberating potential of Osiris, Isis and Horus; as do women. Contemplate the multi-leveled metaphors and symbols this story represents within your own consciousness and body. Remember your Magdalene nature, my beloveds, and be free!"[11]

# CHAPTER 14

## ♣ The Voice of the Magdalenes

The Magdalenes are the unified consciousness of the Magdalene Order available and expressing through many lenses, many voices, many physical self-extensions throughout past time periods such as the Christ drama 2000 years ago, as well as now. Each physical self-extension of the Magdalenes has their own particular challenges to master, as well as unique gifts to offer. The underlying directive for all Magdalenes is to resurrect and ascend separation consciousness. Separation consciousness is essentially crucifixion. It is all the ways we succumb to negative thinking and actions based on fear. This often results in judgment towards self and judgment and blame of others. Each Magdalene (2000 years ago and now) has their own unique voice and way of expressing this directive through their divine mission.

Each Magdalene is here, now, to help raise up the frequency level. We are here to help each other and humanity resurrect and ascend out of limitation, chaos, and negative war-like judgmental behavior and attitudes. The Magdalenes have always been the midwives of shifting the fields of consciousness. That is why the collective power of the unified Divine Feminine consciousness is so important right now.

## Lizbett Shares Her Magdalene Voice

*A greater understanding of what is meant to be a Magdalene in Anna's time can be found in "Anna, the Voice of the Magdalenes," by Claire Heartsong and Catherine Ann Clemett, a sequel to "Anna, Grandmother of Jesus." The following is an excerpt from "Anna, the Voice of the Magdalenes." With the exception of Lizbett, the daughter of Yeshua and Mary of Bethany, Claire brought forth all the characters and their messages with Catherine Ann's asking questions and recording what came through Claire. In the case of Lizbett, the roles were reversed. Claire facilitated Catherine Ann by asking questions and recording so that she could bring forth the voice of Lizbett.*

"CLAIRE:  How old are you now, Lizbett?

LIZBETT:  I am thirteen. I will be fourteen in two more months. Some of the girls are twelve. The oldest is sixteen. Some of the girls in our village have children at our age, but we are on a different path. It is not that we are not allowed to have children at some point later in life; it is just that we are choosing a different training or path of teaching. We young girls, who are coming into our womanhood, are being taught how to carry the information and the codes to a different fruition. We are taught how important it is to be able to utilize our wombs for a higher energetic exchange and a higher alignment with our mates. Whether we do this for our enlightenment or for allowing a greater divinity to come forth when we have our children; it is done with much more loving awareness.

CLAIRE: Did your mother and daddy bring you into the world in this way?

LIZBETT: Oh yes. It was a very sacred exchange, a blessed moment, sanctioned by all the Councils of Light.

CLAIRE: Why do you suppose your mother is called Magdalene?

LIZBETT: She is of that family and that spiritual lineage.

CLAIRE: Does that make you a Magdalene now?

LIZBETT: Yes. Not a fully initiated Magdalene; but a Magdalene at the first level of training.

CLAIRE: Please tell me what your understanding is about being a Magdalene.

LIZBETT: I carry the genetics and the potential for being a Magdalene, which are carried from generation to generation. But just having the Magdalene genetic codes does not make me a Magdalene. There has to be a willingness and readiness of mind, body and soul. Much study, contemplation, and cleansing of thoughts and emotions are required. There are activations or transmissions of spiritual energy that must come down and awaken the codes that are held in the earth elements of the body. Then there can be an ignition of a spiritual fire within. When this happens it ignites internal pathways of knowledge to be expressed in external paths of service. Then you can be addressed as a Magdalene.

Some Magdalenes have to look back many generations to find their genetic connection. To be a Magdalene is not by birthright alone. It is through a deep desire and a willingness to be trained and taught. It is accomplished in collaboration within a lineage of those who have gone ahead of you. It is an honoring of those who walk with you; and it is an honoring of your own physical and emotional self.

When all the required elements are present, there is the uniting of the memory and the ancient wisdom that is carried through lifetimes into the present incarnated self. Then one holds the mantle and the staff of the Magdalene. It is a great honor to never be taken for granted. A Magdalene vows to never bring harm or to feel superior or prideful.

CLAIRE: Are there men who are Magdalenes, or is it only women?

LIZBETT: There are men aligned in a similar order. They are the protectors or knights of the Magdalene. They receive their own similar experience of teaching and fusing higher dimensions of divinity into awakening the codes held within physicality. The frequencies are a little different for the men whose path of service brings together the union of spirit and flesh; but they go about it with a slightly different focus than the women.

It is important to understand that the codes may be carried in a female body in one lifetime and then in a male body in the next. The soul has the opportunity to experience a full spectrum of how the Great Mother, through her Magdalene sons and daughters, helps all living beings return to her full embrace. Some of the Druids carry this ancient wisdom and they work in harmony with those of us who are called Essene-Magdalenes. On certain occasions of teaching and ritual, the men and women come together.

Because there is a slightly different complementary frequency and function, the initiated men and women can come together like a lock and key. There can be a powerful fusion. This is needed for conceiving more awake children in the Light, for conscious dying and rebirth, for the Rites of the Sepulcher, and other things that we do not share with those who would not understand.

CLAIRE: Do you need a partner to have these fusion experiences?

LIZBETT: No. You can do it all by yourself. But it is very helpful to learn in increments with a partner. The partners may change with time, as either one may develop faster than the other, or one may be better suited for a particular ritual and not the other. My parents (Yeshua and Mary of Bethany) and sister (Sar'h) and other relatives were my first partners, like when my mother and I circulated energy with each other. There may be a series of partners, both men and women, until we are ready to be with our partner who perfectly meets our highest destiny.

Then there is a perfect fusion and a perfect fit on all levels. Then we can create an incredible energetic field. There is an energetic interpenetration like a pulse that goes out and then it returns, amplifying and magnifying the joined partners as they join with the Light of the Beloved on High (as Grandmother Nana calls the unnamable God). It is like the sacred triangle. The two people are the base of the triangle and the Beloved is the point at the top, where they both join. They are equally joined at every point of the triangle. Then the triangle becomes a powerful generator of energy like the Great Pyramid in Egypt where my parents took some of their Magdalene initiations. Information and wisdom is gathered and experienced. There is a spiraling out and in of greater and greater magnitudes and more and more dimensions."[12]

### ♥ The Three Mary's Blessing:

*(Myriam of Tyana, Mary of Bethany, and
Miriam of Mount Carmel)*

*(The Three Marys speak as one voice through Claire Heartsong.)*

"Together, as one trinity, we fulfill and reveal what has been held in abeyance for many eons of time. With us comes a company of Magdalenes who also bear witness of the Great Mother and the empowerment of the feminine in men and women. Together we shall lift up that which has been buried and hidden, suppressed underfoot. We shall raise, indeed, our voices as one voice in harmonious unison and exude from the center of our collective heart the fragrance of ascension.

Our voice is as one – the Voice of the Magdalenes. Each of us speaks for one another.

Our merged desire is the healing of the feminine heart and the flowering of this earth – the healing of deserts and the wastelands within souls. Therefore, our vision encompasses men and women walking together as equals, where families, communities and nations honor differences and similarities, allowing and encouraging everyone to express their infinite potential. We see every soul capable of expressing their intrinsic light and bringing forth the highest forms of creativity, each according to their nature and karmic conditions. We also honor and accept choices of limitation. Although these choices may cause suffering, we also know suffering is a divine expression of the Great Perfection. Limitation, as an expression of contrast and choice, has within it the infinite potential to be a catalyst for awakening, compassionate healing and wisdom. Our merged desire is to catalyze and witness the cessation of all forms of suffering while incarnated within our shared human condition.

So we come forth emissaries of the Mother Divine, manifesting as the Christ-Magdalenes, the physical vessels through which she expresses her power on earth. At this time in your day and age there is great need to bring the masculine and feminine into balanced union. By this statement let it be understood that it is never our intention to overpower or cause any aspect of consciousness to become subservient. Ours, at this time of great planetary crisis, is to restore balance to the technologically based mind, which we see as unbalanced masculine energy – for example, the clear evidence that Mother Earth and her creations are dying from all manner of escalating violence, insensitivity, greed and pollution. We experience the masculine mind as bereft and devoid of the feminine heart – the ability, for example, to holistically experience the interconnectedness of all life.

We see that a greater percentage of the Divine Feminine is required. This is why you are hearing so many messages and appearances from the Divine Mother, such as those of Mother Mary. This is the reason books are coming forth, such as the one you are now reading. Because a greater expression of the Divine Feminine is what will bring balance and harmony, we come forth as a female trinity with our beloved Yeshua.

Together we represent the Divine Feminine and Divine Masculine in harmonious union. As a trinity of three women, we exponentially expand the energy of the Divine Feminine within ourselves. Then when we are joined with Yeshua's focusing of the Divine Masculine at the center, there is the co-creation of an encompassing sphere, or an alchemical Grail Cup, in which Mother Earth and humanity may be held. With Yeshua joining us as a fourth force, we also co-create the strong base of a pyramid, by which we "square the circle," and stabilize the unbalanced energies presently multiplying at an exponential rate.

What I have described as "our" stabilizing effort is a microcosm of a universal quantum process, which for this sharing, will not be described in further detail as it is not our intended focus here.

Impermanence, expressing as planetary change, is inevitable. Our desire is to awaken individual choice, based on infinite, intrinsic potential, so that this time of great change may be utilized as an unprecedented catalyst and opportunity for awakening to our individual and collective Infinite Nature. We are choosing to act as a stabilizing agent for this cyclical, birthing/dying process.

We have shared with you the Greater Part of our spiritual work within the Order of the Magdalene; which, whether great or small in its effect, is done on behalf of humanity. Our work is multi-leveled and not easily understood by the ordinary mind. Already it may be dawning within your mind that there was not just one Magdalene but, in fact, many Magdalenes; not just one Mary Magdalene with Yeshua, but three. We know you have questions regarding our personal relationships with each other, our children and Yeshua – a mystery and secret that is in the process of being partially unveiled and told. There is the ripeness now for bringing to light portions of what has been veiled in oaths of secrecy. Even so, for many, what shall be presented will be difficult to hear, much less to integrate. Therefore, we shall bring forth our stories with great mindfulness.

Be at peace, my brothers and sisters. We are the Magdalenes; we carry the gene of Isis to regenerate and bring forth a new genesis, a new creation, and a new "Adam and Eve" – a new generation, a new world and a new heaven. And so it is."13

(A greater elucidation on the subject of the Magdalenes is brought forth in the passage below reprinted from "Anna, the Voice of the Magdalenes" by CLAIRE Heartsong in co-creation with Catherine Ann Clemett.)

### ♥ Anna: The Dispersion of the Seeds of Light

"ANNA: "To a large measure, the voices of the Christ-Magdalenes were silenced and shrouded for 2,000 years. Even so, as I look to your day, the Infinite Light we seeded remains within the genetic codes of your current generations. Gladdened songs of awakening sing from the ancient stones lying deep within the isles of Avalon – the codes of Light vibrate within your blood and bones. The Christ-Magdalenes are awakening and ushering forth a new voice – a song of unity and peace!"14

## Anna's Last Words

"ANNA: Know this, my beloved friend, it is not for the purpose of perpetuating stories that I leave these words; but rather it is for the quickening of the "seeds of the Christ Light" within you. And so it is that I transmit the Beloved's voice so that you may be comforted and know the Peace beyond all understanding. Now it is you, who continues this Great Work for the benefit of all beings."15

# Part 2

## CHAPTER 15

## ♥ *The Beloveds Vineyard*

In 1988, almost exactly a year after my (Claire's) life-altering rendezvous with St. Germain in the Tetons, my consciousness was catapulted into a profound experience of clear light and extraordinary bliss while listening to an audio-cassette called "Urge to Merge." Earlier that same year I had met Allisone Heartsong in Mt. Shasta. He introduced me to St. Germain as he expressed at that time through his full-body channel, Azena Ramanda. I was given an audio recording of a presentation St. Germain had given earlier in Melbourne, Australia. The presentation was called "Urge to Merge." It was while listening to this recording in which St. Germain told of his meeting with Portia in the vineyard that I was lifted up, as if to join them in a timeless space of re-union.

This experience, in which my ordinary mind dissolved into the embrace of the Beloved, was a profound and indelible glimpse that "cemented" my resolve to take the journey into full remembrance of Union and to stabilize that realization in my daily life. I knew that to whatever extent I was able to reach my destination, the journey itself, long or short, was the most important and real offering of service I could give my family and all beings. Whatever would prepare and purify my body, mind and soul to be able to hold, be, and radiate this vast loving energy of Oneness, I was (and am) willing to experience.

And so I embarked wholeheartedly upon the journey into Twin Flame Union. As I shared in Chapter 1, Allisone and I were initiated into the Twin Flame Union process with the catalytic assistance of St. Germain and Yeshua Sananda from August 8, 1990 until August 8, 1991. During this extremely intense year of purification and strict retreat from worldly distractions, I came to know the meaning of Yeshua's words, "Where much is given, much is required." We entered St. Germain's vineyard and we came to know the pressing of the grapes. We came to know how the Vintner makes wine. Though I have tasted sips, I have yet to fully drink of what St Germain calls "the ascended Ruby."

I also came to understand Anna's and St. Germain's true relationship. It was revealed that many years after her conscious departure from Avalon, Anna incarnated as Portia during the time of Francis Bacon. It was she who assisted Francis Bacon to master the physical plane and to become Europe's Wonder Man, the ascension master, St. Germain. And it was because of experiences with Portia in "St. Germain's chrysalis grail" that I came to know Anna as an emanation of the Divine Mother essence. It was Anna/Portia who took me later into the Akashic Records where she and the Magdalenes had hidden their stories to come forth at this time. Anna/Portia is still the Light that shines from my own Magdalene watchtower showing me the way of Union. And it is the infinite compassion of St. Germain and Portia, together with that of other Masters, that keeps my Heart-flame lit and my Heart singing. It is their constant embrace that carries me across separation's ocean of suffering to the farthest Shore.

Having shed many obscuring veils, I am no longer romantically naive about the alchemical process that is required to arouse the butterfly from its sleepy disguise as a caterpillar or its deeper sleep within the tomb/womb chrysalis. As I embody more of the name that St. Germain gave me - "Claire" - I am seeing with greater clarity. I am resting more frequently in the stillness of the "Beloved's Vineyard" where the "going out" and "coming in" meet in simple, ordinary moments of the here and now. Here in the vineyard of Now, I realize I AM the clear sky *and* the butterfly sailing through it - and I AM the magical caterpillar, too!

## Chapter 16

## ♥ *Anna / Portia Realizes Twin Flame Union*

The following is a continuation of the transcription of a "2006 Anna Fireside Chat" with three friends, including Catherine Ann. Because the collective energy was sufficiently unified and receptive, Anna's consciousness expanded into that of her ascended Awareness as Portia, St. Germain's twin-flame. Portia then went on to share her experience of meeting St. Germain in the vineyard and their Twin Flame Union. The last two chapters of Part 2 are variations on this same theme. Although repetitive, the subject is so important for catalyzing the liberation of consciousness at this time that we have chosen to reprint them from the original published material. Many details of the actual process will not be found; but the energy transmissions are readily available to anyone who is ready and able to receive them.

May the words you read and contemplate serve as a vehicle to awaken remembrance of Twin Flame Union. May your journey through the Vineyard be unhindered by obstacles and may you realize a joyful Homecoming for the benefit and happiness of all beings.

"ANNA/PORTIA: I popped into embodiment at the behest of my beloved St Germain after his wandering for 200 years as the so called Wonder Man of Europe. This came about at a time when Germain began to realize that what I had proposed (Twin Flame Union) to him earlier (when he was known as Francis Bacon) was his only hope for the fulfillment of his heart's deepest yearning.

It was only after he had become frustrated with his futile efforts to unify Europe that he began to call me forth once again. He had had a grand vision of assisting the peoples of Europe to know that they, too, could manifest miracles – that they, too, could know physical immortality as he exemplified, that there could be universal peace and harmony instead of conflict and war. But they were just not getting it. And so he became quite disillusioned.

Then within every weary cell of his being he began to call forth his Twin Flame consciousness - that that be I. As he did this, he met with Osiris and Isis, Yeshua and Magdalene and other realized Masters on the inner planes. He became more aware of their cosmic Twin Flame Unions. He realized that by joining with his own Twin Flame energy he could merge with the Twin Flame Union hologram his mentors had accomplished. And so it was that he called me forth and we met on the inner planes. We deeply communed in preparation for my coming into incarnation.

But before I reveal more of this delicious tale, I wish to say a few words about our emerging understanding of Twin Flame Union. The sips of blissful Union we had already tasted caused an unquenchable thirst for more to arise, motivating us to come to the Beloved's oasis - in our case, a vineyard - where we could fully drink from each other's' cups.

We had come to understand there was a ripeness of many resonate souls with whom we had an intimate karmic connection. They were ready to join us once again on the journey of planetary ascension, as they have countless times before. But this activity was going to be on a grander, far-reaching scale than we had experienced with Yeshua centuries earlier. As you know I played the role of Yeshua's grandmother and the mother of Mary. Germain was Yeshua's father, Joseph ben Jacob. We knew that if we realized Twin Flame Union our "flash-point" energy would catalyze the awakening of these brothers and sisters to come forth well prepared to step into their benevolent roles, including realizing Twin Flame Union also in due time.

We knew the "super-nova" energy that would arise from our union would exponentially charge the planetary grids and the genetic codes of all sentient consciousness. An exponential ripple effect would occur, just as it had with Osiris/Isis and Yeshua/Magdalene previously. We were acquainted with the hologram of Union they had been set in place and we knew how to access and merge with it. Now we would completely merge with these beloveds in complete Oneness.

Over the centuries since our Twin Flame Union there continues to be an exponential increase in the number of souls who are able to hold unity consciousness in a relatively stable fashion. This is possible because the additional ascension frequencies our Union set into the planetary grid. Because of this the scales of polarity/duality are beginning to reverse. The status quo agreement humanity has used to hold itself hostage for countless eons is shifting. Fear-based reactive forces are trying to maintain control in the midst of escalating chaos. But their efforts are futile. Inevitable change is making the extremes of polarity even more apparent. Like a leavening agent, this is causing consciousness to rise up from its long sleep. The maturation of souls is quickening. More souls are choosing love, harmony, equality and unity. More and more souls are choosing non-duality consciousness. Increasing numbers, though few compared to the many still imprisoned in ignorance, are slipping out of their chains. I will tell you there is the possibility of a mass ascension. But it will not express in a Hollywood fashion. Indeed, the ordinary mind cannot grasp the nature of the process nor its outcome. In truth it can only be realized on an individual basis. Each soul must choose to cleanse their perception and *experience* the truth that Twin Flame Union already IS. What is required after that will become obvious - in fact, the only reason it has been missed is because it is so very close and so amazingly simple.

Now back to my story. From my vantage point, I knew all was in readiness when every atom and cell of his being began to call me forth. And so it was that I chose to come in and be birthed as a child. I was the daughter of a prosperous vintner whose winery and vineyards nestled in the hills close to where present-day France, Germany and Switzerland come together. Thirteen years had passed since my birth. Then one late afternoon in the season of the Virgin – Virgo, I was walking in my father's vineyard. Some of the earlier grapes had been plucked but there were still quite a few grapes left to ripen before the killing frost. The other laborers had gone back to their abodes. My parents were accustomed to allowing me to linger in the vineyard or to walk freely amongst the fields or to run like a deer over the meadows and hills. They did not worry for my welfare.

The twilight was gathering - the sun was bringing forth its very last glimmerings of golden hues and purple shadows. I slowly walked and paused amongst this particular vineyard's last grapes of the season before they were to be plucked and hauled to the wine vats the next day. Here and there I plucked and lingered with a shiny, deep-red orb, holding it up to the light, smelling of its promised nectar and then placing it gently between my lips. Merging with its essence, I participated with its succulent sweetness. I felt at one with all of my surroundings. The twittering of bird song wafted on a gentle breeze as a lark sang his last fervent love song to his mate before the night gathered all into a stillness.

CW: Juicy details... no pun intended... juicy grapes.

ANNA/PORTIA: The pun is quite intended, beloveds, because you are the juicy grapes the Vintner is gathering to make fine wine – the ascended Ruby.

Now back to my story. I felt a presence, but I did not turn from my celebration of the beauty within my midst and the joy within my bosom. I carried on with the little song welling up in me that I spontaneously shared with the wonder of life all around me. Looking out to the western horizon, I beheld the virgin star that was hovering in the deepness of space, my beloved Lady Venus. Then I heard a foot fall and the rustling of leaves. Somewhat startled, I turned around and looked upon a most wondrous vision of a man. I began to feel an expansion of my heart that left me utterly breathless and mute as I beheld his deeply tanned face and animated lips that were speaking - but I could not yet hear the sound of his words. Then at last I heard a most gentle and kind voice speaking in ways I could barely understand. He looked like one of the laborers, no different really. I thought him to be quite handsome, you know, like any young girl imagines a handsome prince riding a fine steed and going off with him to his magical kingdom without a care or a worry.

As I considered him more fully, I noticed that he was dressed in quite simple clothing. His homespun shirt was rolled up, exposing tanned, fine-boned arms. His wool trousers wore a bit of a patch on the knees. He looked just like one of my brothers or any common laborer in the field, except that his outer clothing didn't conceal his noble bearing. At first I looked fleetingly into his eyes, and then as if I were a moth caught in a flame, we gazed transfixed for what seemed like eternity. Looking into the pools of his eyes seemed as if I were looking into the starlight of the heavens flashing rainbow-colored lights.

I was lost in wonderment as I beheld and sensed what was occurring within my breast. And then this one continued speaking with silver-throated eloquence. He spoke many beguiling words. I noted of him no intent to do harm or any intent to seduce me with sexual ardor. I felt from him an immense fervency – a sense of jubilant homecoming, a sense of relief. I felt an irresistible pull to be close to him. It wasn't the way I felt when I ran into the arms of my father nor was it the way I imagined lovers to be as they melded together in passionate embrace. No, what I was feeling was more like running through the gates to my true Home. It felt very familiar. It was like finding my self – parts of myself that some ancient aspect remembered. It was like some ancient "me" was calling me to enter into the very depths of my being.

Standing before him was like seeing my soul reflected in the clearest of mirrors. It was as if he were there opening me to the very essence of my true Self hidden within my robes of flesh. I had not ever experienced such as this with anyone before. I was in awe as he continued to spiel forth all kinds of wondrous verbiage. Some of it went over my head because I had little education. He went on and on with all manner of lofty words, flaunting my beauty and grace.

Finally it was like – enough! And I said to him, "You know, my dear brother, I am your mirror." And with that he sucked in a deep breath, became speechless and stared into my eyes in wonderment. We stood face to face in silence gazing into each other's eyes as if they were portals into distant realms that held memories beyond this plane. Then he reached out his hand and I took it gladly. There was no hint or whisper that he would take advantage of me. Nor did I fear the continuing darkening of the heavens as the diadems of light pulsed in the blackness of space. The stars shone with a brightness that I had never beheld before. It was as if the sweetness and softness of the vineyard was like a warm quilt gathering us to itself as we walked ever so slowly amongst the grapes.

At the edge of the vineyard was a very large ancient oak tree that seemed to beckon us to pause beneath its immense arms. We settled ourselves on the grasses that grew among the roots of its very wide girth. As we leaned back onto its broad trunk, we clasped our hands together sensing a deep relaxation alternating with a slow but steady upsurge of what seemed like some kind of mysterious urgency. Our breathing began to synchronize as if we were one being receiving and giving of Life's inflow and outflow. Then he pulled me gently into his arms. In this manner we alternated through the night, walking hand in hand or nestled at the foot of the great oak that stood as our witness.

In the moonlight we gazed deeply and steadily into the eyes of our beloved. As our hearts opened, so, too, did the portals of our inner eyes. We began to experience our bodies shifting, becoming more liquid, self-luminous, translucent and ephemeral. A sphere of light encircled us and my sense of a separate self in a body dissolved. I beheld the emergence of many beings of light. I became aware of my beloved

Yeshua. I became aware of Magdalena. I became aware of whirling suns that were dancing and merging and bursting forth as super-nova after super-nova after super-nova. I beheld the creation of suns and worlds and life-forms within ever expanding spheres of creation.

Then we were pulled into the very center of this spiraling dance of stars, worlds, colors and sounds. In the Center we were aware of a great pervasive Stillness. Then there was no center or circumference - just infinite Space - indescribable, unborn, undying, pure radiance - yet there were also continuous, ever-changing emanations of movement, colors, elements, geometries, forms and primordial sounds.

At first we felt nothing but joy and bliss. Then my beloved and I began to feel the immensity of the energies held in the holographic force-fields of separation consciousness, the karmic source of duality perception and the source of humanity's suffering. Our awareness turned to our human brothers and sisters who perceived in fear. We felt their afflictive emotions and the suffering of endless lifetimes that came as a result of their addictive clinging to the deluded perception of being a separate self. We opened ourselves to the suffering of separation in all the realms and dimensions. We began to feel an increasing oneness with every human heart and with the Heart of all sentient life. Timelines of past, present and future met in the present NOW.

We felt the cycles of the earth mother moving through us. On the one hand, we felt an intense contraction of ever-deepening implosion alternating with the feeling of being stretched out into a vast endless expanse. It was as if we were being pulled into a black hole where an immense gravitational force condenses worlds into minute particles no larger than a mustard seed, only to emerge into explosive expansion where subatomic particles dance throughout the immensity of space. And inseparable from this movement and the appearance of forms, there was an infinite Stillness, an infinite Awareness - a calm, compassionate, omniscient awareness. We became the I AM Presence's absolute awareness with a 360 degree point of view.

During the passing hours the moon's silver light and the sun's golden rays merged into a fusion of white-gold – a clear light brilliance. There was no longer reflective darkness nor was there a distinct source of emanating light. With each alchemical pulsation of implosion and explosion, we felt a fusion of our cosmic Twin Flame energy permeating every atom of this earth. The imprint of our Union remains upon the earthplane. Indeed, you can attune to our Union within the holographic codes of your DNA.

At the moment we reached flash-point our physical forms stepped across the threshold into the forevermore. In one another's "arms" we took our ascension into Twin Flame Union.

As you hear or read my words, pause often and listen with your inner ears. You will hear the echoes of our merged love song. Ask for our presence and together, in Oneness, we shall remember Twin Flame Union."[16]

# CHAPTER 17

## ♥ *St. Germain's Story*

### The I AM Presence of St. Germain

*(Note from Claire: For the convenience of the audience assembled at this gathering, Allisone Heartsong (noted as A.H.) poses clarifying questions to St. Germain. It is also to be noted that "I AM Union" is equivalent to what Anna later calls Twin Flame Union.)*

"ST. GERMAIN: So it was that I did come to Terra, even as yourself, for I have loved so grandly this jewel in the heavens which you call your Mother Earth. I have loved this jewel of my breast and the process that you call ascension and the grand design of the Radiant One, the Father/Mother Source, who conceived all of this of which I am part with you in its conception. We have been watching over her for a long time. We have been cuddling the wee ones, nudging and caressing and coming down to touch.

Indeed, the ascension is near and dear to my heart. The evolution of this planet, solar system and galaxy and the universe, indeed, all that has ever been conceived in the void of Mother/ Father God, I love with all my being. And so do you, that is why you are here. And alas, in the grand cycle of your time at the conclusion of what may be called another High-Renaissance, there is once again a desire for a grand enlightenment of the human mind and the establishment of a grander freedom.

So I invite you to relax, to be humored and entertained and allow your doubts and your skepticism, for these, too, are wondrous, and in due time the glass will clear and you will know your SELF as I AM.

So I encourage you to bring all yourself here, every part of you, that I have conversation more fully with my SELF. You are my SELF and I am in profound awe and wonderment as I gaze upon the mirror of you to know more fully who I am. I honor your presence, the beauty that is arrayed before me. You are the jewels in my crown.

In that timing when there was a burgeoning of humankind that desired to know its Divinity, to be no longer controlled and enslaved quite so much, I came forth once again to be a spark and I took upon me grand and wondrous dramas in the courts of Britain and in Europe.

Indeed, my mother was Queen Elizabeth of England[17] who epitomized the colonization of nations, which was part of personal memory of 'star-wars'. Indeed beloveds, it is true - Queen Elizabeth was a grand fiery-haired one, to be sure, with a grand heart and a grand mind and a grand vision and a grand knowingness. She conceived that which be I and she sent me off onto other parentage, the home of the Bacons, where I became quite a boar, as it were.[18]

A.H.: So you are confirming that Francis Bacon[19] was the son of Queen Elizabeth, who gave her son to one of the ladies-in-waiting? [20]

ST. GERMAIN: Indeed.

A.H.: And so you became Francis Bacon?

ST. GERMAIN: Quite a rowdy, to be sure, and not altogether boring. I did gather to myself the ways and means of impressing others in the high places and a way of being quite witty and quite wondrous with verbiage. Yet do you know my beloveds, deep within my soul was a knowingness of who be I. I did have awareness of the design for my coming. The miracles occurred, appearances and 'encounters of the close kind'. When I was yet a youngster, I was made aware, as Francis Bacon, of the knowingness of the ancients and where I had hidden certain treasures. I did find all of that, which was quite exciting - to open the box - the time capsule of myself, and to come into a completion in ascension in that lifetime. I staged the death (of Francis Bacon). That still has some scratching their heads and I continued to work upon the European scene with the grand vision of union, a grand vision to be in the footsteps of that One who was my son, the one you call Jesus.

A.H.: As I understand it, you are saying that even during your youth as Francis Bacon you became aware of soul memory, including your life is Joseph?

ST. GERMAIN: Indeed, not only soul memory, beloved, but that which I had buried in a variety of different places, actual tangible records that I had laid out for myself for a later time.

A.H.: So in the middle of your life as Francis Bacon, you had awareness that you had these previous lifetimes and you had awareness of your mission, including the United States of America?

ST. GERMAIN: Indeed. What the planet was coming into, the shift from the Piscean understanding to the Aquarian and on to the Era of God.

A.H.: ...that you were laying the foundation for that shift?

ST. GERMAIN: Yes, this awareness burned brightly within me. I was entorched with the passion of it and so was that which was my mate, whose name was Portia.

A.H.: And do I understand you to mean that at the end of the life of Francis Bacon an ascension or expansion of consciousness into seventh level occurred that did not involve physical death and reincarnating in a body, but simply staging a false death and burial so that you could continue as the embodiment of Francis Bacon now ascended as a seventh level ascended master and that you moved to Europe to continue as St. Germain?

ST. GERMAIN: Indeed.

A.H.: Approximately how long was it from the time you staged the artificial death of Francis Bacon and moved from England to the European continent, before you met Portia?

ST GERMAIN: We knew one another before.

A.H.: Was she in a physical embodiment or in an ethereal...?

ST. GERMAIN: She was in an embodiment. We knew - she knew better than I - we knew the purpose of ascension was for Union.

A.H.: You mean while you were living the life of Francis Bacon, you met Portia?

ST. GERMAIN: Yes, she, too, ascended in that timing. I thought I was surely the epitome of humility. She let me know that I was not!

A.H.: You said: 'I am the personification of the age of enlightenment.' She said: 'There is more. You can be an ascended Master.' You said: 'I am an ascended Master' and she replied: 'There is more, it is called I AM Union.'

ST. GERMAIN: Indeed. I thought, «Is it not our purpose that we are to transcend all of this and enlighten ourselves and show humanity that what Yeshua did they could do, too? That the miracles he wrought, you could do too? That the grand alchemy of the embodiment, even the bringing forth of flawless jewels, is what you can do too, that you may drink of the elixir of life and be renewed. Is that not enough? Surely, I thought. So I went around for two hundred years in the courts of Europe, exemplifying grand miracles. I was the wonder-man who never grew old.[21]

A.H.: For those who are not familiar with this fact, I wish to mention that there are historical records that St. Germain visited the courts of Europe (England, France, Germany, Russia, Austria, Italy) and people were amazed that after fifty or one hundred years he still looked the same age. He became known as the miracle man, the man who never died, between about 1620 and 1820.

ST. GERMAIN: So, it was not long after the ascension was made and St. Germain was donned as an identity, one of many I assumed, Portia was - the word would be mind-boggling to understand - but she took within her womb a conception to bear forth one who was in ripeness and readiness. Prior to the hour of delivery she had from time to time become quite, as it were, frustrated and upset with me for not choosing the grander part of the visions that she was partaking in. I was not yet quite able to see her vision of I AM Union.

So she saw that in the grand scheme of things I was not allowing into a grand understanding of who she be, so that we might facilitate one another. Now, I did say unto you earlier, how it is that the identity of who we think ourselves to be can be quite tenacious. So it was with that which be I. I was quite taken up with being the ascended Master St Germain and my lofty purpose of enlightening and unifying humanity. In this way, I still clung to separate identity and had not attained full liberation.

A.H.: You were also taken up with the identity of writing the King James version of the Bible.

ST. GERMAIN: That was all before, beloved. Yes, that is true. I was quite in awe of that which be I am.

A.H.: And Portia suggested that there might be more?

ST. GERMAIN: Indeed. She was sort of a thorn in my side, allowing me to know. My beloved, do not get so caught up in this wondrous...

A. H.: ...personification of the age of enlightenment?

ST. GERMAIN: That is a good way to put it. She reminded me, «Do not get so caught up in the enlightenment of the human mind that you forget the greater part. This is but a step into that. It is but a part of the journey, so, my beloved, be you humble." I thought myself to partake of her heart's desire and knowing would limit the manifestation of my vision as I understood it. And Portia looking into the creation of another timing, she did see there would be a ripeness to fulfill her vision. So great was her love that she allowed me the realization of my vision while she withdrew more and more. She was not in anger when she dissipated her embodiment while in childbirth. It was her love, her capacity to allow and to hold to the immaculate concept of yet another birth and another time that released her from that particular drama to bring her forth into yet another incarnation, to shift the tragic to magic.

So, for two hundred years, I was a vagabond and a gypsy upon your plane and appeared quite miraculously without any dust upon my raiment and some exclaimed: 'But you were just in Paris yesterday, and my goodness, here you are in Brussels and there is not a speck of dust on you.' So I did pop in from time to time in wondrous ways to display much wisdom and my understanding of ascension.

There were many who entered mystery schools with me and they became very enlightened, illumined beings.

And so, yes, I had a part to play with others in the founding of this country (U.S.A.). It was my intense desire to create a union of consciousness upon the land, a global community of enlightened beings of full realization of their power Source, no more to be enslaved and governed by any rule that would separate them. I did the best I could in the uniting of European nations into one Europe, but that went awry. I did what I could do to inspire the founding fathers of this, your America, to be the land to receive the dove and the eagle into a merging of a union, to plant the seeds that a race of beings may come forth, an I AM race, America the free.

There is much love in my heart for this. Yet, do you know, my beloveds, when your Declaration of Independence was signed at a bit of coaxing from Uncle Sam (that be I) and your constitutional government was coming into an alignment and the factions were lessening, I was increasingly becoming very dissatisfied in my being . I had a hunger and thirst for something more. I wondered, after all that had been realized at my hand and by those who shared the same vision that I had, why there was such an emptiness. Then I began to remember the invitation that had come to me two hundred years earlier from my beloved Portia.

A.H.: I believe you gave a beautiful demonstration to this planet of what can be accomplished and what cannot be accomplished by an ascended Master making an all-out effort to enlighten humanity.

ST. GERMAIN: Enlightenment can only be done from within.

I chose the greater part and entorched myself so that the Golden Brilliance of the God I AM might radiate and thus entorch every heart of humanity. Like the torch of Liberty (a representation of my beloved Portia), which I inspired to come into creation, I wished to touch and inspire others with the light and song of liberty.

So I decided to come through the back door, so to speak.

A.H.: To move from an individual approach to a universal approach?

ST. GERMAIN: Indeed. I would ask that while we are here that there be the allowing of a grand transmission of an I AM flow so that you may feel of the torch of Liberty I bear. Should you want the More, even as I came to want the More with every cell of my being, then I invite you, too, to begin to ask for full en- torch - ment. And I shall come unto you as your own I AM Presence to stir you, to quicken you, to activate within your heart-seal the Seal of Union.

So it was that there began to be a swelling and a focusing within every atom of my energies here upon your plane. There was intensification beyond comprehension of my desire for I AM Union. I felt a fervent desire to accomplish this with my Twin Flame energy incarnate. You, too, may begin to get the feel of this same desire, for this is the design of your being also. All of humanity eventually will feel what I began to feel.

It was not until every cell of my being was calling forth Union that I removed from my feet the shodding of fine leather that I had worn to enter throne rooms. I released from my shoulders the robes of ermine and velvet. Now it was my turn to enter into my passion upon the donkey of humility. It was time for me to come to know God I AM. It was time for me to release the grand design that I thought I had hoped to fulfill concerning unifying and enlightening Europe - to be in honor of this grand design, to be sure, but to allow the contents of that cup to be emptied, creating room for a grander vision to fill a vaster cup.

So I walked and I went into the inner cities, and I dipped my hands into the sup of poverty and drank of the bitter brew of my less fortunate brothers and sisters. I looked into the eyes of the prostitutes and I went into the prisons of spirit and body and I began to understand myself in a way that I had not done previously. I began to see the twinkle in every eye, regardless of the tragedy, regardless of the drama, regardless of how my brothers and sisters created the illusion that they were victims.

A.H.: You began to feel the Christ in every heart. I would say you were consumed by a yearning for your true home.

ST. GERMAIN: Not just bringing the aspects of myself home that were lovable - those of the light called Christus, but to bring home, indeed, the anti-Christus within my being. To bring all the parts of me Home - the part within me that crucified myself, the part within me that hung on the cross, the part within me that entered into the tomb, the part within me that rose again. I began to see that I and everyone around me was Christus and anti-Christus - was God and Goddess - was I AM. I began to behold the equality and the miracle within it all - in every supporting stone that my feet trod upon and the irritating grain of sand in my shoe; in the rose and in the thorn.

I became humbled and teachable; open and childlike; outrageous in my flamboyancy - my buoyancy, my capacity to bring smiles upon the faces of those who were downtrodden! To be sure I took great delight in being the clear mirror in which my brothers and sisters could have a grander view and reflection of their divinity. I expanded my lens of perception of who I thought myself to be to begin to see through the lens of every point of view of you as I looked through your eyes, walked in your shoes.

At last I began to have an understanding of what I was after and that that was union with the power Source that fulfilled me, that sustained me, breathed me and all life. As I embodied this empowerment I was brought into ecstatic rapture within my every cell. I was ready to bring my Christus and anti-Christus into Union, knowing from the I AM point of view both are ultimately the same energy. In this offering and merging there is ultimate freedom of empowered union - transmutation of all fear.

So it was that I had a great yearning for Home - a yearning for AUM, a yearning for the true gold. Yea, I had been an alchemist turning lead to gold - I thought I knew it all. But now I began to understand the true alchemy that transmutes human fear-based consciousness and brings forth the aura of humanity's greater ascension.

I placed my whole being upon the face of the Earth in grand supplication and yearning. And as I fully released myself to a greater All-Knowing awareness and supreme love - in that moment my beloved Portia came forth and was conceived again to take incarnation. For thirteen years I walked alone, yet, I was not alone, for there was a 'knowingness' that a new star was born.

For thirteen years I wandered about the land, wearing the garments of a laborer, my skin bronzed, and my blue eyes a' twinkle. Then one late afternoon I entered into a wondrous vineyard. It was towards sunset - all was aglow and all the laborers had gone but one. I heard the lullaby of the lark that melted my heart. Through the verdant branches I saw before me the image of a young maiden – classic in her profile, lithe of arm and leg, her hair silken. I was enraptured and in awe. I recognized her. She was caressing the grapes and singing unto each one a lullaby, their rich ruby luster sparkling like gems within her hand, such tenderness, such knowingness, such innocence.

I made myself known unto her and I said: 'Come hither, young maiden.' Then I did avow from my throat, passages that even amazed me. I was so aquiver. A vibration began to overtake me that is not of this world. She said unto me as I sung her praises: 'I am your mirror.' I had not heard this from another before, as this was what I told others. Now is this not a grand knowing for a thirteen-year-old girl? She was a grand wise one. Indeed, she knew what she was viewing and what she was feeling with a great inner wisdom, and in her innocence she was teachable.

So it was as the sun began to emit its radiance among the deepening violet hued shadows and the diadems began to sprinkle themselves across the heavens, that we walked and held hands and allowed a flow, a presence to move within us, to move aside all else, to quicken every atom into all-knowingness. Every emotion, every experience of all humanity, all worlds, all creation poured into us like tidal waves as we held to one another. We became a conduit. We began to understand the true meaning of masculine-feminine, the electro-magnetic energy flow. The Divine Mother of all embraced us and held us in the cup of her heart, else we could not have withstood the experience of such vast energies - it was so intense.

There was not even the whisper of a thought of what could be called a sexual nature that flitted across my mind. What there was an intense circulation - an intercourse beyond imagining that occurred between and through us - both penetrating and being penetrated by the energies flowing unto and through us. All soul memory of the All-That-Is came into our consciousness and our consciousness merged into every atom of the All that IS.

As the sun arose we merged into the light of the Radiant One. That, my beloved, is my body. You are my body. This is my body [pointing to Claire›s body and then touching a nearby rose]. This is my body [indicating the audience all within and beyond the room].This is the Allness that the wondrous teachers of all ages teach. The Radiant One is the home to which we yearn to return. It is an expansion beyond that which the Father/Mother who birthed us before we came into physical form. The Christus is coming to be birthed through you. There is a grand light[22] that is moving through your heavens ever closer in the illusion of time/space. It is raising your frequency. The vibration that you are feeling now is moving you closer to the AUM-stretch, the Source, the Golden Brilliance of the God I AM.

Every step of this process called I AM Union - its involution and evolution, its implosion and explosion is wondrous and to be allowed without resistance which only brings suffering. Every choice of creation is choosing to be divinely embraced by and merged into the Radiant One that I AM. I come as a witness of this ascension - the ultimate ascension to be God I AM. You are star-seeded for this.

So, allow these words to be a spark of re-co-ignition. I love you - I AM you. You are the Radiant One that I AM. In this timing you are the hands and feet that carry the torch of the I AM Presence upon the land. In flamboyant humility be in appreciation of all experience as it comes unto you, for it is you. Allow that Divine Maternal energy to have full embodiment in you so that you may be the Divine Mother unto all your creation. She knows how to relax into the birthing/dying process. Only in this way may the warrior relax and be released of its bondage of illusion that there are two at war with one another.

It is the Mother who knows how to birth the One in harmony and balance.

I bring you tidings of the God I AM, of the Christus within you, the All-Knower within yourself. I would ask before we depart that you allow a moment or two of silence wherein you may all bask and allow this One to enter in if you choose to allow an expansion. You are laying aside your veils and you are entering a new life. Until we meet again, know that ascension is your destiny and you can realize it in every Now.

Namaste, my dear ones."[23]

# CHAPTER 18

# ♥ *Portia's Story*

## The I AM Presence of Portia
## (St. Germain's Twin Soul/Twin Flame)

*(The following material is an edited version of a transcription of the original audiotape which was recorded at a public gathering facilitated by Claire in 1994 in Colorado. Another version is published in "St. Germain: Twin-souls & Soul Mates" by Azena Ramanda and Claire Heartsong. Note that the term "I AM Union" is equivalent to what Anna later calls Twin Flame Union.)*

"PORTIA: As I feel of your hearts in this hour of communion together, do understand more fully who it is who forever embraces you - cradles you - and wipes your wee tears. I come forth to breathe upon you in the silence, in the tenderness of this moment in the form of a story. It is not that you shall become attached to the story or that you shall allow it to become dogma. I do not share it for the purpose that you perceive me as special or that this was something that occurred long ago and does not have relevancy now. Rather it is in listening to the vibrations beyond the words that I desire to stroke you through that which pours forth through these lips to nurture and caress you so that you can remember what it is you have longed to experience. I am here to assist you to know that that for which you yearn is always here in each now moment. It is within you and it is what is perceived external of you.

You are coming more and more into the embrace of remembrance. I desire to assist you in this remembrance through my story so that you will not be quite so afraid of losing yourself in this embrace of Union. Indeed, you shall be more of who you already are, for I shall pour myself into you and as we merge, so shall you remember we have never been separate. So I invite you, dear hearts, and I shall cradle you in these moments that we are together.

Long ago, in what you term time, about four hundred years ago, and plus, the story is set in the merry land of the Angles/Angels.[24]

From the etheric realms I looked down through the dimensions into that which is the Earth. It was during a time of great awakening. It was a time when the land that had previously been very asleep and darkened, was now awakening into a grand dawning.

Ones who previously had laid seed for this hour were taking embodiment again to set forth into motion a movement and a flow that would affect the entire course of events in history - and for the centuries to come. My beloved and I would come forth to pave the way for a new race, an I AM race - a humanity in knowingness of Oneness.

As I looked "down" from my place beyond this dimension, I did behold a magnificent lot of beings. There was one of these who was as myself in male embodiment. I watched over him upon the birthing bed when he was delivered in great secrecy - a great shrouding. There were hushed whispers and dimmed lights when the cries of birthing broke forth through the dry lips of the mother with flaming red hair. My heart ached for her and for the sibling who was born. A young maiden, who was a lady-in-waiting and also a wet-nurse, took the wee babe away, at the mother's insistence, before he even had a suckle at her breast.

The maiden bore him away to a relatively modest cottage; that is, modest by comparison to the room in which this babe was born. The young maiden had married into the Bacon household and she had given forth a still-born child. Her breasts ached with milk and she freely gave of this nurturance to the newborn babe. Upon seeing him the fiery-haired one whispered the name Francis. But it was this loving family who took him as one of their own that gave him the name Francis Bacon.

Years passed and I continued to look "down" upon this lad who had many times been my playmate. There was a longing to romp and play with this one again. He saw me with inner vision and he wished to draw me into his experience, but I said it was not time yet. Other ones, such as myself, who were also in the ethers, participated with me in looking over him. And from time to time they manifested and taught this wee one - the lad with a keen mind, many wonderful things. He opened to awareness far beyond his years or beyond the capacity of those around him, who were indeed great beings. This one had a work to do and it was agreed by the Councils that a great focus of expanded consciousness would express through him to be embodied and exemplified. He would en-torch the entire court of England with new thought, a new capacity to perceive life.

He was a lad when he took a number of grand pilgrimages. He followed the steps of a previous embodiment that he had known as Merlin[25] - one of the Merlins. As an adult there was one with him in the court of England who previously had walked with him as Arthur [26]. There were others as well, who took embodiment to gather again at the great Round Table[27] of consciousness that would draw down the heavens into the Earth vibration. Their work was to lift up the humanity that had been so asleep since the timing of that great One (Yeshua) who sealed his life into the tomb and then arose in an enlightened body.

So, the years passed in the grandeur that was England - the adventuresome spirit of an awakening race. Ships set sail and conquered distant lands. Marriages took place to wed the courts of many nations and to begin a union which was so heartfelt by this one whom I loved.

In laboratories this one secreted himself away with a few others who had a knowingness of the roles they have played in previous eras upon the land. In these secret places there were scores and scores and scores of books. There were vessels that contained elements, herbs and metals of many kinds. For hours and days these ones secreted themselves away. They looked upon the ancient tablets which had survived many wars and the many burnings at the hands of religious fanatics.

These records had been carried and protected by a Brother-Sisterhood through the ages. Some of the texts that most interested my beloved were about alchemy. The time had come to bring forth a grand alchemy beyond just producing gold to be worn upon the body or to bejewel the tables of the high ones in their courts, but to bring forth an understanding of the gold within the human soul. This alchemy of "spirit fire" not only transfigured and transmuted the body to bring forth the elixir of everlasting life but transmuted dualistic perception of the mind. Teachings were carefully transmitted to realized teachers who went forth upon the land. They exemplified what was possible for anyone who chose to enter into these mysteries. And so it was that all who had ears to hear, learned and mastered how they might do this for themselves and for many beings, so that ultimately we may all be free.

So it was that this one, my beloved, was privy to many, many books and records of bygone eras. With the Brother-Sisterhood he went on a number of pilgrimages to Alexandria and other temple sites in Egypt, the Holy Land, Asia Minor, Greece, Italy, Germany, Austria and Switzerland where some of these records had been hidden away. They were vagabonds sealed to one another in fellowship by orders and vows which they honored and perpetuated.

There was a rendering of many histories and dramatic tales steeped with human suffering that were written down and acted out in what are termed wondrous Elizabethan dramas. For it was that Francis Bacon and a collaborative council took the pseudonym, William Shakespeare. After years of being thoroughly stewed and embroiled in much courtly intrigue, my beloved desired a different stage upon which to enact his heart's desire. He was weary of the pettiness and the injustice. Indeed, the judiciaries were, shall we say, on his neck a good bit of the time, and so it was that he desired to withdraw and to participate with humanity in a quieter manner for a time. He wished to come forth in a more empowered manner in which to enact the grand design that was beginning to hatch within his heart.

It was in these last years of Francis Bacon's dramas in the court of England that I made my appearance as Portia. I will not go so much into the story of that particular rendezvous, though it was indeed glorious as we knew each other as divine lovers. Both of us had come into an understanding of what the great yogis of the Far East call the breath of life and how to clear and stabilize energies within the subtle channels of our bodies with our transmuted "sexual fire." We raised our frequency, knew non-duality and lifted ourselves into what is termed an ascended level of consciousness – though I pause here to point out that there are many ascended levels of consciousness. We both staged quite a wondrous release of our embodiments and lives, as we had known them. Our "deaths" were staged and for some, that was quite a relief, and for others there was a knowing that all was well. They knew the greater design.

For myself, there was a growing understanding of an even grander Design not ever forgotten. I had had an encounter in the ethers with my beloved brother, Yeshua; my beloved sister, Mary Magdalena; my sister and mother Isis; and my brother and father, Osiris. I was also introduced to other beings who knew that the cycles of the earth were coming into a consummation at the birthing of the Aquarian Age. We did not know how this would play out but we knew everyone who had ever played a part in holding the patterns of Oneness would arise and come forth to be of service. I knew I had a part to play in this.

I shared my understanding of what I called "I AM Union" with my beloved, but he was not able to fully receive the same vision. It became increasingly apparent that my beloved, while he too desired union, was not yet ready for that which I had come unto the earthplane to accomplish. His dream and vision was to bring forth a union of nations and peoples and a rising of consciousness. His dream was a liberation of the minds that had been darkened for so long, to assist them to know who they be, to follow in the footsteps of Yeshua and to show these ones that all that this one did, they could do as well. I allowed him to freely enter what I perceived to be rather an obsessive adventure as he became Europe's Wonder Man, the one known as St Germain, who lived on the earthplane for two hundred years without aging.

Early on, ten or so years after my beloved donned the name St Germain, when I saw that my beloved was not in a ripeness for Union, I took my leave of the earthplane while giving birth to our beloved daughter.

And so it was that he went on his way with my love always near. For two hundred years he traversed the lands of Europe. As an ascended Master he was not limited to that arena. He sowed seeds in that timing which are now germinating and bearing fruit over this entire planet. It became clear that every effort he was making was being frustrated, even though there was wondrous evolvement and enlightenment. Slowly but surely my knowing of I AM Union gradually became his hunger and his intense yearning to realize.

After the seeding of the United States and her independence from the motherland, my beloved began to grow increasingly troubled within his breast - yes, this is possible for an ascended Master. He began to feel the agony of the sickness that was so rampant upon the land, the suffering of separation, the warring, the diseasement, and the collective disempowerment. When the night was darkest for his soul, he called me forth and I appeared to him in the ethers. We came to know that our hearts' deepest desire could only be accomplished with us both being in physical embodiment and that we required the supportive conditions in which to meet and accomplish our purpose.

In that instant of synergistic agreement my energies stepped down and I was conceived into my mother's womb. I chose to be born in this humble fashion, to be as a child, to embrace all that humanity suffers into my heart - to be no different than you, my brothers and my sisters. I retained the knowing of who I be in ascended consciousness. Angels and beings of light attended me and assisted me to remember why I had come into the earthplane again.

One grand day, just beyond my thirteenth birthday in the season of Virgo, I was in one of my father's vineyards. In this season a bitter early frost had settled upon the vines and the leaves of the grapes had begun to turn. The grapes were full and fragrant and heavy with the ruby. The sun was drifting downward, the laborers had gone to their homes and I delayed my returning to the hearth. The birdsong was so sweet and invited me into a trill and a lullaby as I walked in the midst of the vineyard. I cradled the grapes in my hands and sampled their sweetness. The glory of the sunset was so magnificent on that night. The rising evening star, like a diamond, seemed so close that I could pluck it and place it as a pendant upon my heart.

In that instant, as I reached out to the star, I heard a rustle of leaves and looked across the way and beheld the form of a man. I realized he had been there for some time. I had sensed his presence but I thought it to be ethereal, and so had not turned from giving the grapes my farewell song. Looking upon him, I understood he was not one of the laborers. From a deep place in my heart I did recognize him to indeed be my beloved. He brought himself forth unto me and did extol my virtues. I said unto him: 'My dear brother, I am your mirror.'

Hand-in-hand we walked into the night and we merged the energies of all time and all space into Union.

I wish you to know that he did not take advantage of my

virginity, for that was not even whispered across our thoughts, but we did merge with one another that night in ways that cannot be conceived by ordinary mind. As the sun began to rise, so did we begin to be lifted by the arms of the Father/Mother Source, and we did melt into the Sun/Son of our being. We did birth ourselves anew into the I AM Union that forever is. We did birth ourselves into every atom, into every dimension, into every thought, into every feeling that is the God I AM.

I share with you this story, so that you, too, may be the Mirror unto your brothers and sisters. I invite you to be the Mother's roses and cherished grapes she loves to tend and hold close to her heart as she walks in the vineyard of God. Honor yourselves, love yourselves, deliver yourselves into the majesty and into the frequency of the forevermore that I AM.

I love you. I AM you.

Namaste."[23]

CHAPTER 19

# ♥ *Twin Flame Union Meditation*

## Introduction to the Meditation

Only you can do the Great Work of realizing Twin-Flame Union. Enlightened masters and your soul mate(s) can assist you by synergistically catalyzing the necessary energies; but, it is you who is responsible for your own transmutation and realization process. At some point on the journey, when you least expect it, your cosmic Twin-Flame energy may appear because you are prepared for this experience. Your level of clarity, compassion and karmic ripeness allow it to be so! It is inevitable!

Besides creating a magnetic field that attracts the necessary support for your journey, the most important purpose of this orientation and meditation is to provide you with some easy methods for shifting dualistic perception – the conditioned belief that you are a "self" relating to and needing an "other self" in order to feel whole. This delusional projection is the root cause of human suffering and it is the single factor that prevents you from recognizing and realizing the presence of Twin-Flame Union. The romantic projection of "a one and only ever-lasting true love" dissolves in the embodied awareness that you are already inseparable from your Twin-Flame Beloved.

As you enter into the following meditative process, please know that the Beloved's infinite heart, like the sun, is always unconditionally transmitting awakening and liberating energies – exquisite energies beyond time, form, name, and concept. Eternally present energies that you can now receive if you choose to experience them.

As you listen to the audible words, please deeply contemplate, question, and lightly observe everything that arises during and after your meditative experiences.

For example, witness your mind's incessant parade of thoughts as they arise, fade and arise again. Feel all your feelings – both sensory and emotional – just notice – contemplate without judging or indulging in them or trying to change anything. Remember how, in the past, that clinging and identifying with your passing thoughts and desires caused these subtle energies to coalesce into repeated actions and reactions. Recall how being so fixated and immersed in the resulting dramas caused you to lose the vantage point of being a witness resting in equanimity. Notice how being lost in the story removes the opportunity for awakening as fresh, naked, omniscient Awareness itself.

See how everything in your world continually reflects your hopeful and fearful thoughts and feelings. Observe what you find desirable and how you hope to keep it close. Notice what you fear and push away, avoid and reject – just let it be. Allow your likes and dislikes to unravel as do ethereal clouds dissolve and return into the clarity of space. Contemplate how everything changes and how futile and wearying it is to try to be in control. Have the courage and compassion to acknowledge how painful it is to be held in a prison of mental fabrications – failing to allow phenomena the space to resolve naturally within their true nature. Contemplate all the ways you project and experience your internal world being reflected in your external life. See how your relationship dramas mirror and preserve a fabricated identity that seems solid and real. Observe all the ways you distract yourself through constant busyness. Whether awake or asleep, the mind never takes a break. It doesn't know how to relax and be still. Give yourself the space – just a few minutes without doing or planning anything, to just sit with your mind and become familiar with it. Take out your entire mind's laundry and give it the fresh air of your full attention and compassionate kindness.

Let everything that comes into your awareness be just as it is – inexhaustible energy inseparable from its emanating Source. Like the seamless fabric of waves on the ocean – the waves know they are not separate from their ocean nature – the ocean and the waves are the Ocean waving. Simply be aware, be present for your life and allow the dance of twin-flames – the emanating essence of Life – to be infinite Twin-Flame Union expressing in your body and mind, here and now.

May you experience this guided meditation as an opportunity to let go of the stresses of striving, becoming and redeeming. May you feel supported enough to explore and manifest your life's infinite potential. May you relax your mind and allow what IS to BE self-evident in the flow of your daily life's precious moments. Happy journey! May all beings benefit and find happiness.

Please be aware that by choosing to participate in the following guided meditation that you will be engaging very powerful and transformational energies. Although it is presented at a relatively basic level, this introductory transmission is embedded with keys to multileveled and advanced energy practices. This process is not intended for the idly curious. It is strongly advised that if you wish to use this meditation as part of a regular spiritual practice that you seek the guidance of skilled and authentic teachers.

One such teacher is Tom Kenyon who originally introduced elements of this meditation to me. For those who wish to go deeper and who desire authentic guidance and awakening empowerments, I suggest investigating the various Tibetan Tantric (Vajrayana) Buddhist lineages.

## Twin Flame Union Meditation

If you have not already done so, create a time and a space in which you will not be disturbed. Gather a shawl to keep warm and adequate pillows or a meditation cushion for sitting on the floor or choose a comfortable chair. Adjust the ventilation and temperature so that you can be completely relaxed and comfortable.

After taking your seat, place your hands on your knees or cup them in your lap. Sit up, straighten your spine and allow your chin to be neither tilted too far forward or back. Let the tip of your tongue rest against the upper palette of your mouth. Allow your eyes to be open in a soft gaze or you may choose to close them. Feel free to try any combination of having your eyes open and closed. The point is to be present and aware, while being relaxed in your body – connected to your senses in present time.

Allow your belly to be relaxed as you become aware of your

breath. Breathing in – breathing out. Like a violinist's strings – your awareness on your breathing is not too tight – not too loose.

Audibly exhale any tension until you feel settled – grounded in your body, feeling stable like a mountain. Nothing to do. Nothing to achieve. No expectations. Simply be aware of your breath flowing in – your breath flowing out. Relax into your breathing. Rest in the comforting flow of breathing. When your mind wanders in thought or gets caught in a bodily sensation, notice and simply come back to the awareness of breathing.

*(A minute or so of listening to soothing music.)*

Feeling relaxed and spacious, imagine that you have x-ray vision. Imagine that you can see through your skin into how you imagine your body's organs and bones to be. Penetrate deeply into your bones and enter their crystalline matrix. See the blood cells forming and decomposing in your bones' innermost marrow – emerging and dying, like infinite numbers of stars bursting into light and dying into darkness – numberless cycles of galaxies, universes and beings coming into existence and nonexistence – into the seamless, inseparability of form and formlessness.

Feel into the vastness of space within each cell of your body. Imagine the unfathomable distances between each atom and each atom's subatomic particles. See, hear and feel the dynamic creative energy bursting into form and dissolving back into space. Feel this blissful energy as it comes forth and recedes again and again. Allow childlike wonder and curiosity to carry you deeper into the vast infinity of space that surrounds and is within you – that is you. Notice that there is a gap between your inhales and exhales; and how the nature of this gap is space. Linger and rest in the space of still awareness.

Breathe this awareness into your skin – into your sense of being a separate self. Breathe spaciousness and permeability into your body – what you have thought to be quite solid and desire to be real. Be completely naked, transparent and open to being a much more expanded and fluid identity – a being of light that is more space than composite particles – a being that is free of all limitations.

(*A minute or so of listening to soothing music.*)

Now silently breathe in the creative seed syllable "OM" and sense your body expanding until you are the size of a solar system or galaxy. Breathe out "OM" audibly into the furthest reaches of space. Relax into the reverberations of "OM" going out and coming in with your breath. (*Pause.*)

Slowly and silently breathe in "AH". Allow your body to shrink and become the size of a mustard seed. Shrink further into the size of an atom – the size of a subatomic quasar beam. Audibly breathe out "AH" into the furthest reaches of space and then deeply relax into the reverberations of "AH" going out and coming in with your breath.

(*Pause.*)

Silently breathe in "HUM" and go into and beyond any sense of quantifiable inner space. Audibly breathe "HUM" out into pure space. Allow the outflow and inflow of "HUM" to become softer and more subtle, dissolving the boundaries of inner and outer. Relax and rest in merged, naked, still awareness.

(*A minute or so of listening to soothing music.*)

Breathe and flow into the awareness of things arising and floating in space. Flow into the awareness of space being inseparable from things. Breathe and let go of your moorings – merge inner and outer – above and below – masculine and feminine. Experience your heart's speechless bliss as you come into the awareness of union and emptiness. Feel the infinite love flowing through your heart as it emanates, sustains and welcomes back the whole of creation dissolved into Homecoming. Be this vast, all-encompassing Source of Love and inseparable Awareness.

(*A minute or so of listening to soothing music.*)

Experience this loving consciousness, which is your own true nature, now taking the form of any beloved, enlightened Master in whom you feel a great trust, upon whom you can completely rely and in whom you can take complete refuge. This luminous being of rainbow light now stands or sits in the space in front of you. His or her body, clothing and adornments are experienced to be real, but are not solid. Allow your imagination and awareness to bring forth as much detail as possible. Or simply rest in an awareness of a brilliant orb of light and the presence of a great love.

(*A minute or so of listening to soothing music.*)

Now become aware that above his or her head is another luminous being whose form is even more ethereal and radiant. These luminous bodies are inter-penetrating emanations of a vast, formless, omniscient consciousness – the cosmic Twin-Flame Beloved which is beyond any point of reference. Imagine these emanations to be perfectly aligned upon a self-luminous column or pillar of inexhaustible light.

Allow these enlightened, infinitely compassionate beings to witness your intense longing for union and liberation, not only for yourself, but for all suffering sentient beings. Turn your mind to your heart's longing for these Masters of Light – your Twin-Flame Beloved – to be inseparably present in your life – present in your very being. Bring your open heart to this Source of great love and healing. Allow your feelings of gratitude and love for this expression of your Twin-Flame potential to rise with intense clarity and feel this same love and gratitude for you pouring forth from your Beloved's heart.

(*A minute or so of listening to soothing music.*)

Now bring your awareness to the Master of Light – your Twin-Flame – before you and notice a very bright, pulsating sphere of white light radiating from the Master's forehead at the third eye point between the eyebrows. Allow this radiation to enter your third eye. Allow the cleansing and empowering white light to fill your head and entire body. Experience all forms of physical obscuration being absorbed and dissolving into white light. (*Pause.*)

Bring your awareness to the Master's throat where a radiating, clear ruby-red sphere of light transmits a penetrating red ray into your throat center. Experience all obscurations of enlightened speech and masterful creativity to dissolve into the vibrant, ruby-red light which flows from your throat into your entire body. (*Pause.*)

Now bring your awareness to a sphere of scintillating, sapphire-blue light in the center of your Master's heart. Allow the transmission of a clear blue light to enter and fill your heart and slowly spread throughout your body and mind. Allow the Master's all-knowingness to be absorbed into every cell and experience all ignorance dissolving into deep, sky-blue clarity. Allow the Master's infinite mind to merge with your mind.

(*A minute or so of listening to soothing music.*)

Now allow your awareness to encompass all three lights simultaneously. Experience the merging of the white, red and blue lights until they become one purifying violet flame encompassing your entire body. The violet flame cleanses and dissolves every obscuration that covers the true nature of your enlightened body, speech and mind.

As this purification occurs, allow your entire body, speech and thoughts to merge with those of your enlightened Master Beloved in front of you who embodies your Twin-Flame energy.

Rest in this experience of merging totally and completely with your enlightened consciousness.

(*A minute or so of listening to soothing music.*)

Imagine now that directly above the crown of your head your Twin-Flame energy is manifesting as a series of interpenetrating beings of ascending, subtle light. Feel your immense love and gratitude for the purifying and empowering stream of blessings which flow freely from them into a tube of light that connects directly into the crown portal at the top of your head.

Imagine this vertical central channel extending downward in front of the entire length of your spine. Allow the spheres of colored lights and the accompanying energies to flow into this inter-dimensional channel where they come to rest in potentiated stillness inside your body. The Master of Light – your Twin-Flame Beloved – now completely dissolves his or her form into a stream of clear, nectar-like, white light which descends into your central channel. Your Twin-Flame energy completely merges with you in an experience of heart opening, oneness and lucidity. (*Pause.*)

You have glimpsed your full enlightenment potential. The journey now is to complete the purification process so that you can stabilize all your glimpses into the continuity of full Twin-Flame realization.

Rest completely in this experiential glimpse of oneness and let this momentary transcendence assist you to continue your journey into Twin-Flame Union. Make a promise to yourself and your Twin-Flame that you will walk this illuminating path in humility and harmlessness.

Dedicate this rare and precious experience to all beings so that they, too, may experience liberation and happiness. Perhaps you can take a few minutes to imagine all beings experiencing their Twin-Flame energy above their heads and having an experience of loving oneness and healing peace.

*(A minute or so of listening to soothing music.)*

Now slowly bring your awareness back to the flow of your breath and the sensations of your body. Move your fingers and toes. Be aware of your body as it is sitting in this here and now. Please remain seated and allow your experience to integrate slowly before moving away from your cushion or chair. Take a few more minutes to breathe normally. Rest in silence. Allow this experience to gradually open the doors of nondual perception and guide you into masterful action in your daily life.

*(A minute or so of listening to soothing music.)*

May joy, prosperity and well-being always arise as you mindfully and skillfully move your energy through your remaining days. May you realize how precious your life is and not waste this opportunity. See yourself as being the loving and compassionate Twin-Flame master of light you have always desired to come into your life to love you. And as you do this, know your Twin-Flame Union will manifest into your awareness as surely as does the sun at the return of dawn.

Peace be with you.


A recorded CD of this meditation can be found at the back of the book.

# Endnotes

[1] Claire Heartsong, *Anna, Grandmother of Jesus*, S.E.E. Publishing, Copyright 2002, pp. 300-301

[2] Catherine Ann Clemett, *Soulweaving, Return to the Heart of the Mother*, LightRiver Media, Copyright 2014, p. 265

[3] Claire Heartsong, *Anna, Grandmother of Jesus*, S.E.E. Publishing, Copyright 2002, pp. 79-83

[4] Claire Heartsong, *Anna, Grandmother of Jesus*, S.E.E. Publishing, Copyright 2002, pp. 83-84

[5] From "*BECOMING: 2011, Awakening the Great Human Potential,*" Anna material copyright by Claire Heartsong, translated and published in French by Ariane Editions, Inc., Montreal, Canada. info@ariane.qc.ca Reprinted from the original English by permission of Ariane Editions.

[6] Claire Heartsong, *Anna, Grandmother of Jesus*, S.E.E. Publishing, Copyright 2002, p. 84.

[7] From "*BECOMING: 2011, Awakening the Great Human Potential,*" Anna material copyright by Claire Heartsong, translated and published in French by Ariane Editions, Inc., Montreal, Canada. info@ariane.qc.ca Reprinted from the original English by permission of Ariane Editions.

[8] Claire Heartsong, *Anna, Grandmother of Jesus*, S.E.E. Publishing, copyright 2002, p. 85.

[9] Claire Heartsong, "A 2006 Anna Fireside Chat" Excerpt, S.E.E. Publishing, Copyright 2010 Conversation with three friends including Catherine Ann Clemett

[10] Claire Heartsong, "A 2006 Anna Fireside Chat" Excerpt, S.E.E. Publishing, Copyright 2010 Conversation with three friends including Catherine Ann Clemett

[11] Claire Heartsong, "Anna Gathering" Excerpt, S.E.E. Publishing, Copyright 2006, Anna Channeling Session, Santa Fe, NM

[12] Claire Heartsong and Catherine Ann Clemett, *Anna, the Voice of the Magdalenes*, S.E.E. Publishing, Copyright 2010, pp. 218-220.

[13] Claire Heartsong and Catherine Ann Clemett, *Anna, the Voice of the Magdalenes*, S.E.E. Publishing, Copyright 2010, pp. Foreword 26- 28

[14] Claire Heartsong and Catherine Ann Clemett, *Anna, the Voice of the Magdalenes*, S.E.E. Publishing, Copyright 2010, Foreword, pp. 319-320

[15] Claire Heartsong and Catherine Ann Clemett, *Anna, the Voice of the Magdalenes*, S.E.E. Publishing, Copyright 2010, pp. 361-362

[16] Claire Heartsong, "A 2006 Anna Fireside Chat" Excerpt,

S.E.E. Publishing, Copyright 2010 Conversation with three friends including Catherine Ann Clemett

[17] Queen Elizabeth, (1533-1603) daughter of Henry VIII.

[18] The boar was one of Francis Bacon's signature codes.

[19] English Renaissance philosopher Francis Bacon (1561-1626).

[20] A lady of rank who is a member of the royal household and in attendance on a Queen or Princess.

[21] Voltaire (real name Francois Marie Arouet, 1694-1778), French author and philosopher, reports having met and conversed with St. Germain at several occasions and describes his appearance as that of a man of 45 years of age. When meeting St. Germain again 40 years later, he expresses his puzzlement at St. Germain's unchanged appearance, still looking 45 years of age.

[22] Reference pertains to the photon belt

[23] Azena Ramanda and Claire Heartsong, *St. Germain: Twinsouls & Soul Mates*, Queensland, Australia, Triad Publishers, Copyright 1994, Reprinted by permission of Triad Publishers, pp. 133-148.

[24] England

[25] Magician and seer, helper of King Arthur.

[26] Reference is to Arthur, King of Britain and hero of the Round Table; supposed to have lived in the sixth century A.D.

[27] The large circular table at which King Arthur and his knights used to sit, giving its name to an order of knighthood instituted by the King.

# Bibliography

Claire Heartsong, *Anna, Grandmother of Jesus,* S.E.E. Publishing, Copyright 2002

Claire Heartsong and Catherine Ann Clemett, *Anna, the Voice of the Magdalenes,* S.E.E. Publishing, Copyright 2010

Catherine Ann Clemett, *Soulweaving: Return to the Heart of the Mother,* LightRiver Media, Copyright 2014

*"BECOMING: 2011, Awakening the Great Human Potential,"* Anna material copyright by Claire Heartsong, translated and published in French by Ariane Editions, Inc., Montreal, Canada. info@ariane.qc.ca Reprinted from the original English by permission of Ariane Editions

Claire Heartsong, *"A 2006 Anna Fireside Chat"* Excerpt, S.E.E. Publishing, Copyright 2010 Conversation with three friends including Catherine Ann Clemett

## APPENDIX A

## *Claire's Acknowledgments*

With eternal gratitude I wish to acknowledge the Source of these teachings - Anna, St. Germain and Portia - without whose constant Presence, blessing and compassion this book could not have come forth. I also wish to acknowledge all the friends who have contributed to and supported Anna's benevolent work in so many ways over the years. Special thanks go to Catherine Ann Clemett for envisioning this book, initiating its compilation, encouraging my involvement in its completion and preparing its publication and distribution.

From my deepest heart, I also wish to express my love to my beloved twin-soul, Lorenzo, for his clear awareness of Union and his deep commitment to sharing the journey as a conscious couple - no matter how intense our burning in the Beloved's alchemical furnace - our unified voice proclaims, "YES!"

# *Catherine Ann's Acknowledgments*

I am grateful, first of all, to St. Germain for being the catalyst for so much to come forth in my life in directions I would never have fathomed. I am also grateful as well to Anna, Portia (the Oversoul of Anna), and all the Councils of Light along with St. Germain and the other Ascended Masters that are ever guiding this grander picture far beyond what us humans can even truly perceive, to unfold.

I am thankful to Claire Heartsong for all the information and channeling she has brought through over the years; as well as for making available the previously published chapters of the meeting of Portia and St. Germain so that they could serve as the core of this book. I would also like to acknowledge my co-author of *Finding the One True Love: How Changing the Rules Will Change Your Life*, Angelina Heart, for her support and for her pioneering work, immense wisdom, dedication, and teachings on twin flames from which I have learned so much. And lastly, I wish to acknowledge and honor my own twin-flame, the *Beloved* within for bringing this awareness and this unfolding of twin flame understanding forward in me consciously. I honor and bless you the reader, and your twin-flame, as the alchemical marriage and catalyst for Oneness to occur.

# Appendix B

## *About the Authors*

### Claire Heartsong

Claire in a Dartmoor faerie glade, Devon, England

While raising a family, Claire received a Masters degree in fine art and art education. She taught art as an adjunctive faculty member of Boise State University until her spiritual path took her to Mount Shasta, California in 1989.

Claire channeled the book, *Anna, the Grandmother of Jesus* which was published in 2002 and has also co-authored its sequel, *Anna, the Voice of the Magdalenes* with Catherine Ann Clemett. Her travels sharing Anna's message have taken her into the embrace of spiritual family world-wide.

She is presently enjoying living a quiet contemplative life with her spiritual partner, Lorenzo, in a remote and beautiful, wild mountain-river valley located in the Shasta-Trinity National Forest of northern California.

Since the sequel was birthed and published in 2010, Claire has been devoting her time to entering more deeply into meditation practices and conscious relationship as a path of spiritual awakening. This is embroidered with the delights of Nature and co-creating simple projects with Lorenzo. They enjoy combining their mutual love of inspiring prose with his passion for nature photography and her visionary art.

## Catherine Ann Clemett

Catherine Ann has been on a spiritual path her entire life although this did not come into the forefront for her until her late twenties. Her early life was devoted to training, performing, teaching and choreographing dance which culminated in her receiving a MFA in Dance, Drama and Theater from the University of Hawaii in 1978. Her professional dance career abruptly ended as a result of injuries sustained in a car accident. Although devastated by this at the time, it opened the way for her to shift her focus to more spiritual endeavors studying with many teachers, channels, and healers over the years.

Besides being an author, Catherine Ann has trained in many different light work and healing modalities as well as being certified as an Integrative Coach with Debbie Ford, training in past-life regression with Dolores Canon, and being certified in hypnotherapy through the American Association of Transpersonal Hypnotherapists.

Catherine Ann is committed to bringing an awareness and resurgence of the Magdalene Order back on the planet. In this regard, she travels the world as an international workshop leader and speaker; facilitator of planetary grid activations and tours; and a hypnotherapist.

As a free spirit; traveling, writing, developing seminars and workshops, and engaging in her passion, Argentine Tango and other ballroom dance, is now where Catherine Ann is focusing her attention these days.

# APPENDIX C

# LightRiver Media Products

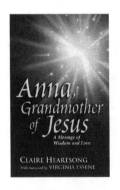

### ANNA, GRANDMOTHER OF JESUS

By Claire Heartsong

Meet Anna, the extraordinary woman who birthed a Spiritual Lineage that changed the world! In the late 1980's Anna, an ascended being also known as St. Anne, appeared to Claire saying no one knew her story. She asked Claire if she would be willing to write the story of her life as Anna. Fourteen years later this remarkable book emerged fulfilling Claire's promise to be the conduit for Anna sharing about her life and experiences. Understand the important role of the Essenes at Mount Carmel in supporting the holy family and the other crucial participants in the Christ drama. Understand the important role of the Essenes at Mount Carmel in supporting the holy family and the other crucial participants in the Christ drama.

### ANNA, THE VOICE OF THE MAGDALENES
By Claire Heartsong and Catherine Ann Clemett

In this book, the sequel to *ANNA GRANDMOTHER OF JESUS* by Claire Heartsong; through a regression process facilitated by Catherine Ann; Anna and eighteen other Magdalene adepts and initiates bring forth intimate messages about their lives in France and Britain after Jesus' (Yeshua's) resurrection. They disclose their personal and deeply transformational experiences with the resurrected Yeshua, which occurred over the course of many years. Discourses on a variety of spiritual topics are offered, including material which some may consider heretical and controversial. Long-held secrets are revealed in such a way as to assist the lifting of the suppressed Divine Feminine/Magdalene voice in our time.

Both Anna books are also available in French through Ariane Editions Inc. www.ariane.qc.ca. Books are currently being translated into Spanish as well.

### SOULWEAVING,
### RETURN TO THE HEART OF THE MOTHER

By Catherine Ann Clemett

"This is so much more than a book - rather it's a gateway to accessing your True Self. By intimately sharing her personal journey; the breakdowns and breakthroughs, Catherine Ann has developed 12 powerful tools to use to access one's True Divine Nature. This book has truly touched my heart in an absolutely profound way. Every chapter is rich with pure wisdom and insights. This book is a powerful catalyst and 'must read' for anyone on a conscious path of Spiritual Awakening. I consider this book to be one of the most significant publications that I've ever read, right up there with the Course In Miracles."

*- Jean Trebek, Studio City, CA*
*(Science of Mind Practitioner and wife of Jeopardy Host, Alex Trebek)*

### *HOW TO FIND THE ONE TRUE LOVE: WHY BREAKING THE RULES WILL CHANGE YOUR LIFE*

By Angelina Heart and Catherine Ann Clemett

*Honorable Mention winner in the*
*2010 Writer's Digest International Awards.*

Has true love eluded you? Do you feel like he or she is out there somewhere just waiting for you...if you could just figure out how to connect? You needn't have a broken heart, feel lonely, or be alone anymore. Save years of frustration, embarrassment and futility resulting from projecting your ego's false interpretation of love onto another.

### *WHAT EVERY HUMAN MUST KNOW TO SURVIVE & THRIVE ON PLANET EARTH*

By Virginia Essene

Renowned author, spiritual pioneer and channel of guidance from the higher realms, Virginia Essene now shares about the acceleration happening on the planet, within your bodies and within your societies. Due to the urgency in present human consciousness, the spiritual realms are vitally concerned about the critical aspects that humanity has not yet fully attained. *What Every Human Must Know* reveals the major concepts essential to all of us for making the smoothest and safest transition through the present "ascension-of-sorts" that the planet and all of humanity are undergoing right now. Now, discover what you can do to thrive amidst this acceleration and change, getting answers to questions you may not even have known to ask.

### *BLESSINGS FROM THE HEART OF THE ROSE ORACLE DECK*

By Sheila Murphy

Blessings from the Heart of the Rose is a 44 oracle card deck and 166 page guidebook. This divination tool assists you in entering the sacred space of your soul essence within, where you carry ancient truths and the keys to your own intrinsic knowledge. These cards help you connect into the mystical marriage of the divine feminine-divine masculine union; the path of oneness. Each card is a stunningly beautiful individual work of art, containing light codes and esoteric symbols beckoning you to enter into the deeper mysteries of creation. The rose, a symbol of the Christic energy of love, deeply connects you with realm of the heart in concert with the earth kingdoms and realm of faerie. Each card offers a dream, a visual story, a journey and a blessing to remind you that you are intricately part of the interconnected weave of life.

## Other Products and Services From
## LightRiver Media

LightRiver Media offers many other spiritual, metaphysical, Twin Flame and self-help books and audio mp3 downloads. Go to: http://lightrivermedia.com for more information on:

- Books, card decks, and audio downloads
- Regression sessions or other readings with Catherine Ann Clemett
- Workshops and Seminars
- Magdalene Grid Activations
- International Trips and Tours

For more information on the above, please visit:

http://lightrivermedia.com/services.html